OREGON LAND

Rural or Urban?

The Struggle for Control

Wayne A. Leeman

Millwright Press ■ Ashland, Oregon

Printed in the USA
Book design: Sara Patton, Maui, HI
Cover design: Lightbourne Images, Ashland, OR
Cover photo: Simone Garlaund, Ashland, OR

Publisher's Cataloging in Publication
(Prepared by Quality Books Inc.)

Leeman, Wayne A.
    Oregon land, rural or urban? : the struggle for control / Wayne
A. Leeman.
    p. cm.
    Includes index.
    Preassigned LCCN: 96-94975
    ISBN 0-9654913-2-3

    1. Regional planning--Oregon. 2. Rural development--Oregon.
3. Land use, Rural--Oregon.   I. Title.
HT393.07L44 1997   307.1'4164'09795
                                    QBI96-40568

CONTENTS

iii

Contents

To my brother, Richard

PREFACE

Supporters of Oregon land law contend that it is the best in the nation. Yet it has not achieved the objectives of those who enacted the law. It has not prevented "sprawl." It has saved little farm and forest land and it has preserved little greenspace. At the same time, it has left users of land deeply frustrated — farmers who would like to build a house on their land for their grown children, farmers who would like to retire and sell their land for urban development, young men who would like to begin a career in farming on small acreage, retirees who would like to live on a few acres at the edge of town and low-income workers who find housing expensive.

The crucial 1973 legislation and its administration have given rise to a large number of government officials at both the state and local level (a "bureaucracy"). It has stimulated a great deal of litigation and led to the growth of a profession of land-use attorneys and land-use consultants (experts in the law who try to help individuals get around its manifold obstacles to action). If enactment of the law has not preserved farmland, forest land, and greenspace, what has it done? It has created massive obstacles to the optimal use of land, it has raised the price of land and housing, it has slowed down economic development and deprived people of jobs.

The very objectives of the legislation can be challenged, as I will demonstrate in Chapters 4 and 5. Evidence that farm and forest lands need to be protected is almost non-existent. And the cost of Oregon land law is high, the cost of goods and services forgone, goods and services that might have been supplied on urban land.

I am an economist. As an economist, I am interested in scarcity. And land, the solid surface of the earth, is scarce. In my analysis of the consequences of scarcity in land, I try to stay close to the facts. I have talked to land-owners, rural and urban, realtors, land-use attorneys and consultants, and government officials concerned with land.

My book is economics in prose, not in diagrams and equations. (The geometry and the algebra of supply and demand are implicit in the words, and economists will have no difficulty in identifying them.)

It is hard to believe, but true, that the basic 1973 land-use legislation was passed with virtually no consideration of its economic consequences. Equally hard to understand is how subsequently more than two decades could pass with no economic analysis of the law and the land-use regulations that followed. My book is the first thorough and comprehensive study of the economics of Oregon land-use law.

I hope that I have maintained a measure of scholarly detachment. But after a lengthy study of alternatives in land-use policy, I find myself with a distinct point of view, one that puts me at odds with many in the environmental movement. Although I am aware of scarcity, I am not a Malthusian. I do not think that men and women will starve, or that the prices of food and fiber will skyrocket, because cities are developing on what has been farmland.

Actually, I consider myself a moderate, one who usually finds himself in the middle of the road. In Oregon, and elsewhere on the West Coast, however, the debate on environmental issues is skewed to the left. Environmentalists seldom consider the role of the individual in conserving and increasing the wealth of the community, and they seldom look at the limitations of government. They perceive a moderate in matters of land-use as a conservative, if not a reactionary.

I guess that I must be a conservative liberal, an old-fashioned liberal, much interested in technology, in growth, and in markets (albeit markets with carefully designed governmental constraints that deal with monopoly and spillovers). For me, economic development is the only way that we may hope to lift the burden of poverty from humanity.

Environmentalists advocate a large role for the government in the preservation of greenspace. Because I have much to say about the value of free choice, the role of free markets and the limitations of government, an inattentive reader might conclude that I consider individual choices always to be better than collective decisions. This is not my position at all. I recognize that individual choices often are parochial, fail to take account of adverse consequences for adjacent landowners (adverse "neighborhood effects") and frequently are properly constrained by governments that represent the community.

A few words about the huge influence of the environmental movement. When environmentalists talk about spillovers (like air, water, and smoke pollution), or when they advocate the governmental preservation of unique sites, they are on solid ground. A market economy, in the absence of regulation, does not deal adequately with non-market interdependencies and with natural monopolies.

The owners of a steel mill do not take into account the costs they impose on neighbors when their mill spills smoke over the surrounding countryside. A private forest company, seeking to maximize profit, does not consider the downstream consequences of felling trees along the banks of a river. The adverse consequences of spillovers, of "neighborhood effects," represent serious failures of the market.

Because the preservation of land that one day may be incorporated into public beaches, parks or greenways is fraught with both market and political risk, private enterprise has little hope of reward for such acts of civic virtue. It leaves to government agencies most efforts to preserve land that is unique.

The commendable insistence of environmentalists that governmental agencies limit pollution, along with their efforts to preserve particular sites, has provided them with a following. They have carried that following over into their efforts to preserve and conserve farmland and forests. But they and their followers are not aware that the environmentalist position on a comprehensive preservation is poorly thought out. Environmentalists do not consider the costs in forgone development of resources that are not put to use.

I am, then, an environmentalist when the issues are spillovers and the preservation of terrain that is exceptional. I find myself in opposition to the environmentalists when they unthinkingly fail to take into account the costs of a generalized preservation and conservation. Potential readers of this book should keep this in mind before they reject its message as that of a black reactionary who cannot appreciate the color green.

Any consideration of efforts to preserve greenspace must face one unlovely reality. Within the preservationist movement are many smug, self-righteous, self-centered people: Smug as they contemplate their own surroundings. ("I like my town the way it is.") Self-righteous in their environmental morality. ("I am virtuous whereas developers and farmers who want to subdivide the land are greedy, as are the householders who would eat up farm-land in order to live at the edge of town.") Self-centered in their unwillingness to share. ("Latecomers from California can go somewhere else to live.")

In this book, I consider five models of land use. The first I call "historical sprawl." It allows development with few constraints, but presents problems when newcomers intrude on the space and solitude of early arrivals (Chapter 6). The second is a flexible urban growth boundary that moves only after opponents and supporters of a change wage costly fights in hearing rooms and courts (Chapter 7). The third is a rigidly fixed urban growth boundary that would make land and housing horribly expensive (Chapter 8). The fourth, a greenbelt, is a compromise that might be acceptable to moderates (Chapter 9). The fifth, orderly sprawl, may also be acceptable to moderates. It will appeal to advocates of affordable housing, and to advocates of free choice who at the same time want protection for households that seek out empty space and solitude (Chapter 10). In chapters that precede and follow these models, I deal with the issues and principles that divide opponents in the struggle for control of land.

· · ·

No work of intellectual inquiry is performed alone. Over the several years that this book has been in progress, many individuals have contributed to its production.

I would like to thank John R. Hassen, land-use attorney. He read critical parts of my manuscript, raised challenging questions, and supplied knowledgeable answers to difficult questions. Both his editorial suggestions and his views on content were invaluable. Richard Stevens, land-use consultant, likewise read material and patiently taught me much about the application of state regulations to the use of land in Oregon. Lyle McLaughlin, developer, provided encouragement and knowledge as I struggled to understand the complexities of real estate development. Elizabeth Fujas equipped me with insights into the economics of small-scale agriculture. These people and others are members of 20-20 Commitment, an active, non-profit organization in Southern Oregon, devoted to the improvement of public policy in matters of land-use and regional planning. At its regular Wednesday-morning breakfasts, its members did what they could to educate me. They put up with occasional heresies (like my contention that some free-market allocations of scarce land are less than optimal).

Curt Weaver, land-use consultant, taught me a great deal about the early implementation of state land-use legislation in Southern Oregon.

On hikes with the members of the Sierra Club, I found out about the worries of environmentalists. They listened to me patiently and sought to penetrate my stubborn skepticism about parts of the environmentalist agenda. Oriented toward science, they will, I hope, read with care a scholarly inquiry into the relationships between a human economy and the ecology of non-human species.

My brother, Richard K. Leeman, generously shared his impressive knowledge of computers and his abilities as a writer. With a great deal of careful analysis, he did much to improve the organization and content of my key chapter on environmentalism.

Patricia Bigford proofread the entire manuscript and supplied much useful editorial advice.

In the end, I take full responsibility for errors of fact and interpretation that survive in this book.

CHAPTER 1

INTRODUCTION: BOUNDARIES AND SPRAWL

Land, over the centuries, has been a source of conflict. Who controls its use? Who decides?

As they wandered through grasslands and woodlands, hunters and gatherers held the land in common. Territorial disputes were between tribes. In time, cultivators claimed exclusive use of parcels, and private property in land emerged for village housing, workshops, and commercial activities.

Individuals bought and sold land. They erected barriers to prevent unwanted incursions. Good fences make good neighbors. They went to court to settle disputes over ownership and boundaries. (Some peasants in Europe walked their boundaries with their neighbors once a year to minimize future disputes.)

Even as private property in land came into existence, community ownership of land remained. Livestock was pastured on the commons, and trade fairs were held on public land. Roads and streets, traditional routes for transport and commerce, were held in common. Church groups owned land for buildings and cemeteries, and governments owned land for administrative structures.

Governments exercised the right of eminent domain to take land for community use; courts required them to pay fair market value as compensation.

As population grew and more and more people lived in cities, spillovers (neighborhood effects) became a problem. Weed seeds blew on to neighboring fields. Unsanitary conditions on private lands spread disease to neighbors.

In the absence of regulation and zoning, those who could afford it bought land "for protection," acreage that kept their neighbors at a distance.

But those who lacked the funds to purchase large holdings or were reluctant to move away from irresponsible neighbors put pressure on local governments to regulate behavior. City Councils passed sanitation laws, noise ordinances, weed ordinances, laws to deal with storm water, and so forth. They began to create zones for particular uses — industrial zones, commercial zones, zones for multiple-unit housing.

In recent decades, a relatively new issue in land use has emerged and this is much of what my book is about.

SPRAWL

Local populations grow (a result of new births and immigration from other parts of the country). Inner cities decline. Traffic congestion and limited parking become problems. Crime becomes an issue. Families move out into the suburbs and acquire a second car. Expressways are built, and shopping centers.

With the emergence of suburbia, environmentalists worry about the loss of farm land, forest land, and open space. They are supported by newcomers to an area who do not want others to follow them into their peripheral retreats. The person of modest means does not have enough money to buy land for protection against intrusive neighbors. So he turns to government to protect his sparse-ly populated neighborhood from further incursions. He likes the idea of an urban growth boundary that keeps other people from crowding into his rural retreat outside the city limits.

At the same time, however, a potent market emerges for land and homes at the edge of the city. Many families want to live on large lots or small acreage. Developers are eager to build structures that meet these preferences. The authorities respond to voter preferences for better arterial roads and automobile-friendly shopping centers.

A major conflict arises: Preservation vs. Growth. Pro-tect the land, preserve farm, forest, and open space. Or, spread out, use the land, develop the economy—provide jobs, increase income and wealth, supply resources for consumption, manufacture, commerce, homes, and social services. Environmentalists (preservationists and conser-vationists) tend to be Malthusians, fearing increases in population in a world of "finite" resources. Advocates of growth are more optimistic, anticipating increases in the productivity of land, labor, and capital, and forecasting continued technological progress.

The conflict also becomes one over lifestyle. Those who are avid to preserve greenspace advocate life in a compact city: small yards, privacy fences, mixed neighborhoods of homes and small shops, travel on foot or by bicycle. Resi-dents who want to see substantial green can go to a park. Open space is to be communal, a "new commons," sought by those nostalgic for the old village green.

Advocates of a growing city, on the other hand, prefer that people be free to choose a low-density lifestyle. They believe in *private* open space.

Finally, the conflict comes to a dispute over compen-sation. Private owners of farm and forest lands contend that they should be compensated for their loss of develop-

3

ment rights. This is the "takings" issue. May a community that enacts new rules and regulations effectively take away the value of private property, and do so without compensation?

The conflict between preservationists and partisans of growth takes several forms. Should urban growth boundaries be fixed or expanded? Should land be kept in agriculture or should it be made available for home-building? Should more arterial highways be built, or should resources be put into sidewalks and bicycle paths? Should automobile travel be encouraged or should the automobile be tamed? (The environmentalists do not choose to speak of taming the *drivers* of the cars. They ignore the preferences of the people driving or riding in autos. For them the automobile itself has volition.)

Environmentalists reject the historical pattern of the American frontier, where individual farmers did what they wanted with their land and where independent businessmen promoted the growth of their towns and cities.

One of the most fascinating participants in this modern *kultur-kampf* is the farmer. He wants to protect agriculture as a way of life, protect it from the incursions of suburban neighbors. But when he gets old and unable to farm, he wants to get top dollar for his land by selling out to developers. "Scratch a farmer," say the environmentalists, "and you get a subdivider." (But what happens when you scratch an environmentalist? Might you get a self-interested person quite willing to increase the value of his or her existing home through restrictions on the supply of competitive buildable land?)

Equally fascinating is the appearance of the "neo-traditional" in landscape design and architecture. Land should be laid out in the old-fashioned grid system, with narrow streets, sidewalks, and old-fashioned alleys. Homes are to be built with porches. Automobiles will be tamed with

4

narrow streets and numerous intersections. Residents are to walk to the neighborhood grocery and bicycle to the nearby coffee shop.

Look carefully at the large following that the environmentalists have built up in the suburbs. The average suburbanite is green, but only a pale green. When he finds himself sitting in a traffic jam, however, or reads about crime downtown, he remembers that he is an environmentalist, and concludes that his city must hold population in check. He has found his place at the edge of town; now he wants to shut the door. It is a form of NIMBY, not in my back yard. Other people have to live somewhere, but let it not be in my edge-of-town neighborhood.

The environmental movement has something to do with attempts to preserve farms and forests. But it also has a great deal to do with preserving the lifestyle of those who settled in an area first.

FROM ANARCHY TO ORDER

Men and women interested in how people are distributed on the surface of the earth may advocate free choice or they may seek control. Early participants in the movement for planning, like Ebenezer Howard and Patrick Geddes, drew on Prince Kropotkin, the anarchist. Kropotkin wanted people to be free and he favored "countless small farms," small-scale agriculture. His words read like the words of a present-day advocate of low-density development on the edge of cities. "Have the factory and workshop at the gates of your fields and gardens."[1] Others concerned with the spread of cities were the opposite of anarchists. They pushed for control. Le Corbusier, who favored municipalities with 700-foot office towers and six-story residential apartments, argued

5

that the design of cities was too important to be left to its citizens.[2]

Present-day plans likewise may provide for choice or be designed for control. When freedom of choice is valued, people are free to live downtown or free to live on large lots or small acreage at the edge of the city. When control is the objective, people are required to live in a compact city of small lots and high-rise apartments, and go to a public park for the enjoyment of trees and grass.

Ultimately, this book is about control. Who decides? Who decides how land is to be used? Individuals or the community? Developers or County Commissioners? Local officials or a state agency (in Oregon, the Department of Land Conservation and Development)?

I hope for a compromise, a middle ground that leaves considerable choice to the individual but within acceptable constraints imposed by the community.

CHAPTER 2

ENVIRONMENTALISM: FROM SPILLOVERS TO PRISTINE NATURE

Senate Bill 100, enacted by the Oregon legislature in 1973, set the stage for present-day land-use planning and controls. In creating the powerful LCDC, the Land Conservation and Development Commission, the legislature was responding to serious concerns about the environment. In 1968, Paul Ehrlich had published *The Population Bomb*. In 1969, a huge oil spill had occurred on the coast off Santa Barbara. About the same time, Governor Tom McCall told the legislature that "an urban explosion of environmental pollution is threatening the livability of Oregon in such a manner that effective land use planning and zoning have become a statewide, not merely local concern." In 1970, the first Earth Day was held. And in 1972, Donella Meadows and others had published *The Limits to Growth*.

Oregonians were worried about municipal and industrial pollution on the Oregon coast, pollution of the Willamette River, and the loss of farm and forest land to development. They were resonating to the voices of the environmentalists.

ENVIRONMENTAL VALUES

Environmentalists firmly adhere to a particular set of values.

Environmentalists value open space — farms, forests, and small towns — with only a few rural residents. Most environmentalists value a sparsely populated world, which means that they favor restraints on increases in local, regional, and national populations.

Then, the most dedicated environmentalists put a high value on a pristine nature, a nature undisturbed or little disturbed by men and women. Human beings are not considered to be part of nature. Dedicated environmentalists prefer a world with few or no human artifacts (buildings, dams, reservoirs, aqueducts, and the like). They value wetlands, tidal flats, old growth forests, and species diversity. They are determined to protect existing species. "Wild birds and animals," says one worker for a nature conservancy, "have as much right to this earth as I do." Individuals devoted to the protection of wildlife do not care to be identified with the animal rights activists, whom they perceive to be part of the political right, but they are in effect firm defenders of the rights of non-human species.

Environmentalists value very much the preservation of resources for the future, resources that those presently alive can use in their later years and resources that will be available to future generations.

As a means to the preservation of open space, pristine nature, and resources for future use, environmentalists are attached to slow growth.

And then, that which perhaps gives them their strongest claim to support from the general public, environmentalists value a healthy environment for human beings — things like clean air and water, and sanitary disposal of waste products.

SPILLOVERS

Environmentalists point out that private enterprise frequently is a source of pollution.

Spillovers (pollution of air, water, and soils with smoke, noise, toxic wastes, and so forth) have long been recognized by economists as one kind of market failure. Pigou, in the 1920s and 1930s, called them "externalities", factors external to the market. I prefer, however, the more expressive terms, "spillovers" or "neighborhood effects". Smoke spills over into a neighbor's property. Chemical fertilizers spill into rivers and hurt people downstream.

Human activities often adversely affect non-human species. They reduce or even wipe out the habitat of the spotted owl or the marbled murrelet.

The environmentalists are on solid ground when they address neighborhood effects. The unregulated capitalist market does not adequately deal with them. Manufacturers, farmers, private forest companies, and others often fail to consider spillovers when they make decisions to produce and trade. A steelmaker maximizes profit by ignoring the damage that his smoke does to the neighbors. A private forest company maximizes profit by ignoring the consequences of felling timber next to a stream. Profit-oriented businessmen often ignore the impact of their actions on the environment. The community then acts through government to regulate and control spillovers. The United States has an Environmental Protection Agency to deal with such matters. Oregon has a Department of Environmental Quality.

To be sure, environmentalists often fail to consider the costs (relative to the benefits) of checking spillovers. Near the end of this chapter, we will look at the high costs of trying to preserve a pristine nature, and then we will look at a compromise, an approach that strikes a balance between attempts completely to subdue nature and attempts to place nature totally off limits.

. . .

Along with activities to check spillovers, environmentalists advocate the preservation and conservation of resources.

Goals 3, 4, and 5 of Oregon's Statewide Planning Goals deal with these subjects. Goals 3 and 4 are drawn up to preserve farm and forest lands. Goal 5 is to preserve energy sites (natural gas, oil, coal, hydro, geothermal, uranium, solar and others), and preserve water areas, wetlands, fish and wildlife, scenic views and scenic waterways, and recreation trails. Groundwater, minerals and aggregate resources are to be conserved. Much emphasis in Goal 5 is placed on the preservation of *open space* — defined as lands used for agriculture or forests, and any land that would protect air, streams, or water supply, or conserve natural or scenic resources, soils, wetlands, beaches, tidal marshes, historic sites, and golf courses.

Frequently, those who drafted these statements of goals, use the word "conservation" when they mean "preservation." Careful analysis requires a distinction between the two words. A resource may be *preserved* indefinitely, permanently, kept available more or less in its present state — a lakefront beach, an old-growth forest, or a historic battlefield. Or a resource may be *conserved* for a finite period of time, then used in production — copper in the ground, say, or timber standing in a forest.

PRESERVATION OF UNIQUE SITES

Environmentalists can argue persuasively for the preservation by government of certain unique sites — waterfront lands, parklands, ancient forests, or perhaps the best site for a school that will be needed in the future.

They can point out that distant parkland or distant beaches are poor substitutes for nearby sites when the costs of travel or transportation are prohibitive. Governments may buy such lands and keep them out of less desirable uses.

To be sure, it is possible that private businessmen and women may act to preserve lands for parks, schools, or civic structures. A shrewd businesswoman may recognize that in a few years the community will want to place a school on a certain site. She may hold it off the market and keep a less desirable structure from being built on it until a school district needs the land. However, a private action like this carries both market risk and political risk. The business person may make a bad forecast. Or when the government is ready to buy, it may choose not to pay fair market value for the property, using its power of eminent domain to get the land for a low price. The cost of going to court to get proper compensation may be deemed prohibitive.

Owners do want compensation when the community insists that an individual or a private enterprise give up rights of use.

So mostly a community must rely on governments to preserve unique sites. But while the case for government action to preserve these sites is a strong one, the arguments for government action to engage in widespread preservation of farm and forest land are weak. For one thing, there is a great deal of farmland and forest in the United States and abroad. Landowners near any particular piece of farmland deliver products that compete with its output. And the products of distant lands arrive by road, rail, or ship to compete with locally produced output. Certainly there is a great deal of timberland in the Pacific Northwest capable of delivering wood products to market.

In Chapter 4, I discuss Thomas R. Malthus and his erroneous forecasts of food shortages, and, in Chapter 5,

I look at early Twentieth Century Malthusian anxieties about timber famines.

Environmentalists may be shocked at my cavalier dismissal of the goals of preserving farm and forest. What about all that natural beauty to be found in the countryside and in distant forests? In the final section of this chapter, I deal with the value judgments and the economics implied in the preservation of pristine nature.

Now we need to look at *conservation,* the desirability of setting aside resources for a fixed period of time.

CONSERVATION

The economics of conservation is little understood. Many people consider conservation to be self-evidently a good. Benjamin Franklin tells us that a penny saved is a penny earned. But saving in itself does not add to income. Had Benjamin Franklin spoken with greater precision, he would have asserted that "a penny saved *and prudently invested* adds to earnings in the future." A thrifty man saves, and if that man wants to increase his wealth, he also invests.

Conservation, like saving, is prudent. But simply holding an asset and waiting may not be the best stewardship of wealth. In the case of forests, Benjamin Franklin might have put it something like this: "Under some circumstances, it would be a good idea to save (conserve) a forest. Under other circumstances, however, it would be better to cut down the trees immediately and replant, or harvest the timber and put the land to use in urban pursuits."

Much of the time, it is better to use resources than to conserve them. Utilizing land, raw materials, and labor, factories turn out consumer goods and capital goods. Construction firms build factories, office buildings, highways, streets, residences, and structures for suppliers of

12

services — schools, theaters for plays, concert halls, stadiums, hotels and motels for travelers, and docks for fishing boats.

Surprising as it may seem, private owners often conserve resources. Environmentalists frequently think that only governments engage in conservation. If the expected value of, say, petroleum twenty years hence is greater than the cost of holding it underground, the owner does not lift it. If the future expected value of farm crops is high, the farmer-owner does not sell his land to a developer. He keeps the land in agriculture, perhaps for the benefit of his grandchildren. If the future value of timber is high enough, the owner of forest land does not harvest it.

Environmentalists need to look more clearly at the role of markets and trade in the well-being of human beings. A free market economy gives people choice. Money, the medium of exchange, is a bearer of options. Dostoevsky called it "coined freedom." Markets provide choice in consumption goods, in capital goods, and in material inputs (cotton or wool, copper or aluminum, wood or steel). Markets give people a choice in where they work, where they live, and what land they occupy. Householders are prepared to pay for housing that they like, and businessmen are prepared to pay for desired commercial space, office space, or space for manufacturing. The expenditures that developers incur for raw land reflect the choices of people who want to dwell in town or in the countryside, or the choices of businessmen who want to supply the goods and services that people purchase.

Markets promote growth. They increase consumption goods, capital goods, and service capacities. The industrial revolution, revolutions in commerce, the revolution in computers — all contribute to increases in the standard of living.

The developer of land is an important player in the free

market. He represents the *future*. He represents people who want to live in larger or better homes; he represents children or grandchildren who will want jobs and want to live in the area in which they grew up; and he represents people who want to come to the area from outside.

Trade, buying and selling, are the way households satisfy many, if not most, of their preferences.

The forecasts of the private sector as to future demands are likely to be better than similar forecasts of government officials, the reason being that the former are betting their own wealth on their forecasts and decisions. Putting one's money on the line concentrates the mind; it sharpens one's sense of the future. Officials are gambling with public funds. The personal consequences of error for these people are small, particularly when the outcomes on which they are betting are not expected to occur for 50 or 100 years in the future.

But, says the environmental community, market prices do not adequately measure future needs for resources. Government, as representative of the community, should conserve forests and other resources. Environmentalists insist that the government do more than concern itself with spillovers and acquire unique sites. They want government to conserve resources that they believe would otherwise be severely depleted by the actions of profit-oriented individuals and enterprises. They fear a grim future, one without critical timber, water, mineral, and petroleum resources.

When a conservationist refuses to accept private-market forecasts of the future supply of resources, he is sure that he, or a carefully selected planner, knows better what the future will bring. But past forecasts of catastrophists have been wrong. Pessimists have been forecasting for decades that we will run out of oil and that oil prices will skyrocket. Proved oil reserves are now large enough to supply the world for 43 years at current rates of production, compared with 1970s estimated reserves of less than 35 years.[1] Real oil prices have been falling over time. And then pessimists have forecast that with the destruction of farmland, we will all go hungry. But world markets are burdened with farm surpluses.

Evidence is lacking for the belief that legislators or planners have a clearer notion of the future than private market-oriented individuals. It is not clear that the governmental representatives of the community can better forecast the future availability of minerals, fossil fuels, and land. Government officials, and their constituents, may be irrationally afraid of the future and fail to consider the prospects for improved technology in agriculture or the development of alternative fuels and substitute materials.

. . .

We must examine one more reason why government officials, under pressure from the community, err when they decide to conserve resources. They fail to *discount* future benefits and costs. We need to look at the role of the interest (discount) rate in decisions to conserve resources.

FAILURE TO DISCOUNT THE FUTURE

Resources that are conserved for the future are not available for use in the present. They are available neither for early consumption nor are they available for early growth-enhancing investment. Conservationists seem not to care about early benefits, or the lack of them.

In contrast, a sophisticated private investor uses an interest rate to discount future returns. He knows that use of a discount rate will maximize growth in his wealth. Failure to discount anticipated future interest or dividends will put him in investments that grow slowly. Late returns can be reinvested only at a later date.

The conservationist does not believe that a similar approach should be used in public sector decisions. Use of a discount rate may be all right for the capitalist, he says, but he does not accept market prices and interest rates as indicators of appropriate public policy.

Environmentalists, however, have thought little about the role of interest rates in government decisions. To be sure, some have come to recognize that the big dams in the Western United States were constructed by agencies that used excessively low interest rates in their justification. So they favor high discount rates in such decisions. But they do not recognize that interest rates should also be used in decisions to conserve resources.

Perhaps this omission is not so surprising. While many people understand the role of the ordinary, regularly used, interest rate in decisions to invest, relatively few understand the importance of the discount rate in decisions to conserve, although in both cases the decision-maker is concerned with future values.

If they do consider discounting in decisions that deal with minerals and forests, conservationists want a low rate or a zero rate of discount. They argue that failure to save these resources will lead to catastrophe. They know that a high rate of discount on future returns would lead to an early lifting of oil, to an early harvest of timber, and to early production of other non-reproducible or slowly reproducible resources.

The case for a high rate of discount in decisions to conserve, however, is strong. Future uses do not help people now. The present use of resources contributes to a higher standard of living in the present. Copper now is more valuable than copper thirty years hence. It holds down the costs of appliances now. Timber and building sites available in the present hold down the present cost of housing.

At this point, the reader may want to skip to Chapter 5 and read the section "Discount Rates and the Cost of Timber Conservation." Foresters use discount rates all the time, and examples from forestry are a good way to see how they work. Most people know something about the power of compound interest in the increase of wealth. Serious advocates of conservation need to understand the power of compound discount in deciding between present and future uses of natural resources. This power can be seen most clearly in forestry, where timber companies deal with 40-year or 100-year harvest cycles.

Discount future returns, insists the economist. Find out present value. Not only does the present use of resources contribute to a present-day standard of living; it contributes to a future standard of life. Resources available for present use can be invested in the present, can be invested now rather than later. Resources can be invested in equipment that turns out consumption goods in the future, equipment, for example, that reduces the labor of women in the household (washing machines, vacuum cleaners, dishwashers, and the like). Iron ore mined today can be installed as steel beams in factories, factories that provide consumer goods or capital goods. Such early investment contributes to economic development. If, alternatively, ore is conserved, present-day iron ore will be higher priced, steel will be higher priced, fewer factories will be constructed, and a smaller quantity of consumer and producer goods will be turned out. The economy will grow more slowly.

Conservation not only deprives the private sector of goods in the present; it deprives the public sector of early resources. An economy that is growing slowly has less wealth and less income that can be taxed. Consequently less resources are available for the public sector — sewers, treatment plants, streets, bicycle paths, parks, bridge safety, buildings retrofitted for earthquake safety, toxic-waste clean up, education, medical care, poverty and mental health programs, facilities for care of the elderly, and so forth. An electorate in a stagnant economy is reluctant to vote for resources to help the disadvantaged.

Look at this matter in another way. Suppose today a great deal of farmland and forest land was rezoned for urban uses. Thirty, forty, or fifty years from now, Oregonians would deliver less farm and forest products to market. However, an urban use of the land would lead to a higher rate of growth, and, through a higher growth rate, people in Oregon would have at their disposal some combination of the following: more energy, more labor saving devices in their homes and places of work, more and better medical facilities and services (because more resource would have been devoted to research), more and better transportation (perhaps more mass transit), and more leisure. They also would experience less pollution and have less toxic waste to clean up; more resources would have been made available to deal with spillovers.

I am not arguing against conservation. What I am saying is that conservation has a cost. The cost of conservation is relinquished alternatives in the present. It is forgoing use of resources in the present that could be used for the present production of consumption goods and for the present, growth-enhancing, private and public capital goods.

The cost of conservation is best measured with a discount rate that gauges the value of present goods over future goods. Because the discount rate is a measure of the cost of conservation, decision-makers can make rational choices only if they discount the anticipated value of goods proposed for conservation.

The study of time in economic analysis, the study of decisions to produce or conserve, is indeed difficult. As stated earlier, the reader may choose to skip to Chapter 5 and read, "Discount Rates and the Cost of Timber Conservation." The examples offered there may be helpful.

Because the market rate of interest represents individual preferences, the liberal-left is likely to advocate a low "social rate of discount," one which reflects community preferences and recognizes the importance of conservation. It will argue that individuals are short-sighted and inadequately consider the well-being of future generations. Skeptics, on the other hand, will contend that individual preferences as to present and future should be given a lot of weight, and they will ask whether a public official or a planning body is likely to have a superior knowledge of the future. They may point out that private enterprise also is trying to see what the future will bring, and, because it stakes a lot on its forecasts, it may try harder than public officials to get them right.

Moreover, affluent environmentalists, trying to persuade its government representatives and officials to act in the name of conservation, may be overlooking the immediate needs of the poor. The poor person is concerned more with food and improved housing for his family today than with taking care of his not-yet-born grandchildren and the unborn heirs of his affluent neighbors. The affluent advocate for a low rate of discount has to argue that the needs of future generations are more important than washing machines for poor people today and more important than improved housing for the poor. That resources conserved for the future deprive people of present benefits may not matter so much to the well-off resident in the suburbs. It matters a great deal to the low-income person who is not eating well and living in low-quality housing or even living on the street. His or her standard of living is lower than it might be because the government has decided to limit lumber production and protect agricultural land, perhaps out of an attachment to thoughtless conservation.

One more point concerning future times. In all likelihood, future generations, even without massive conservation, will be better off that those presently alive. Growth in the past improved the lives of people. Growth in the future probably will do the same.

A few years ago, Lawrence H. Summers, then chief economist of the World Bank, pointed out that future generations probably will be more affluent than present generations, and that those alive today might be better off to use resources in the present rather than conserve them for the future. Our grandchildren, he wrote, probably will better off than we are. Recognizing that nobody can predict accurately long-term growth rates, he asked his readers to recall that standards of living today are three times higher than 60 years ago in the United States, seven times higher in Germany, and almost ten times higher in Japan. He then put forth a rhetorical question: Should his American grandparents have reduced their standard of living, when lives were materially less attractive than now, in order to leave raw materials in the ground for his benefit?[2]

If future generations are likely to be better off than present generations, then conservation transfers resource from the poor to the rich, from less well-off generations in the present to anticipated better-off generations in the future.[3]

Once again, I am not arguing against conservation. I am insisting that for a good balance between present and future, decision-makers, private and public, should consider the cost of conservation and should use a discount rate that reflects that cost.

The Land Conservation and Development Commission in Oregon is responsible for development as well as conservation. Yet in its goals, there is no mention of a discount rate. There is no recognition that failure to discount future resources slows down the rate of growth. But, in fact, there is an implicit discount rate in the Goals of LCDC. It is a zero rate. LCDC believes that resources conserved for the future are just as valuable as resources available in the present. It does not recognize the role of the discount rate in achieving growth.

As we look at the case for widespread preservation and conservation, we come to recognize that environmentalists, in failing to take into account future growth possibilities, are pessimists.

OPTIMISM, OR PESSIMISM?

The advocate of growth is more hopeful about the future than the environmentalist, believing that grounds for pessimism are weak. He points out that some resources, while finite, are so abundant as to be nearly inexhaustible — iron, aluminum, silicon, magnesium, titanium, manganese, nickel, carbon dioxide, oxygen, and hydrogen.[4] Then, with an adequate supply of energy, substitutes can be developed for resources that are really scarce. Aluminum can be substituted for copper, ceramics for steel, nickel for cobalt, glass for tinplate. One analyst writes of a "principle of infinite substitutability." He argues that society might subsist on inexhaustible or nearly inexhaustible minerals with only a small decline in living standards. An economy then would be based mostly on glass, plastic, wood, cement, iron, aluminum, and magnesium.[5]

The market has performed well in the past in developing new resources. When people feared the exhaustion of whale oil, mineral oil took its place. After the obvious sources of petroleum were identified by surface seepages, men developed sophisticated techniques for locating concealed oil reserves. In time, petroleum engineers learned to drill five miles underground for oil and also to drill deep below the ocean floor. Scientists and engineers learned to extract metals from ores with low metallic concentrations. And, as we have already seen, they found numerous substitutes for natural materials.

For the production and utilization of these substitutes, energy is the critical item. Mankind can count on a 400-year or 500-year supply of coal. It seems likely that long before coal is exhausted, scientists and engineers will have developed an inexhaustible, non-polluting source of cheap energy as a substitute for depleted fossil fuel. Men will rely on one or more of the following — energy from fusion, energy from the breeder reactor, solar energy, geothermal energy.[6]

The conservationists do not explain why, in the future and suddenly, the market will no longer function as it has in the past, will no longer function as a mechanism that motivates people to look for alternatives.

Harnessed by free market, improvements in the technologies of agriculture and wood products have held the Malthusian dragons at bay.

SCARCITY AND THE COSTS OF ENVIRONMENTAL PROTECTION

A surprising number of environmentalists reject economic considerations in matters of environmental protection.

Economics is a study of scarce resources and alternative ends. Environmentalists talk much about scarcity (scarce land, water, old-growth forests, birds, mammals, and so forth) and say much about resource exhaustion. For them, the word "finite", used frequently in their statements, is virtually a mantra, suggesting an absolutely fixed supply. Decrying the relevance of economics, they do not understand the significance of scarce means that have alternative uses. Scarce land, forests, and other natural resources can be used in different ways for the achievement of different goals. A tree may be used as a nesting place for birds, or it may be cut down and used for lumber. Which is the best of these and other alternatives? A serious environmentalist cannot escape economics.

Scarcity is the source of cost and *cost* to the economist is "opportunity cost," the cost of forgone alternatives. What will consumers forgo if the community chooses to save a tree for bird life? Or what will the community forgo if the law permits a tree to be cut for lumber?

When considering environmental constraints on the market, the analyst should take into account the costs, in forgone alternatives, of these environmental constraints. When environmentalists eschew economics, they ignore what people have to give up if they decide to conserve a resource.

Sometimes environmentalists object to cost-benefit analysis because of its technical difficulties. The big obstacle is the problem of measurement, particularly the measurement of benefits. It is difficult to measure the value of clean air or clean water. Critics argue that market prices are a poor measures of benefits and costs. Prices in a capitalist economy, they contend, reflect individualism rather than community welfare, reflect the preferences of individuals rather than the "common good".

The case against dubious measures of benefits and costs is a strong one. Along with a good many fellow economists, I am skeptical of far-fetched efforts to assign numbers to phenomena like biodiversity. But that does not mean that those who decide on matters of spillover prevention or conservation should ignore the costs of such activities. Even when numbers are not available, interested private parties and officials should insist on a *description* of the costs of any proposed action.

Suppose an environmentalist testifies that we must not cut a stand of trees! A legislator reviewing the proposal might ask, "If we do not harvest the timber, would we not be giving up lumber that could lower the cost of homes for the low-income segment of the population? Or dwellings for hard-working members of the middle-class who would like to live on the edge of a forest?"

Decision-makers must consider costs particularly when trying to achieve the final increments of desired benefits. The earliest improvements in air or water quality provide large benefits in improved health and quality of life. They might easily justify high costs. But the benefits of getting rid of the last bits, the final increments, of impurity in air or water are much less.

All this is economics, and environmentalists will find it hard to deny its relevance in decisions to conserve.

How about the contention that the *price system* is useless when efforts are made to quantify the benefits and costs of environmental concerns? Because it measures only *individual* preferences and costs, the price system, it is alleged, fails to deal with the common good.

But for most people, individual or household preferences are real, and important, and many, if not most, people would say that this reality ought not be ignored on grounds that a particular decision is alleged to represent the good of all. A low-income householder wants a better home for his family — a newer house on a larger lot, one that is not crumbling because its old wood is rotting away, one that is insulated against cold drafts and the hot temperatures of summer. A poor person would like a better-paying job, a "family-wage" job, perhaps in the timber industry.

An affluent member of the upper middle class may decry these individual preferences as he sits in his well-insulated, air-conditioned house and looks out at his spacious lawn, but he is a bit of a hypocrite if he argues that the common good (the existence of a far-off spotted owl) should completely override these concerns of less well-off families.

Let me, once again, list some of the costs that might be incurred when conservation is encouraged. In order to protect the environment, individuals and the community may have to forgo consumption and capital goods, education, child welfare, care of the aged, a higher standard of living for the poor, family-wage jobs, mental health, earthquake preparedness, rebuilt inner cities, and much more.

Environmentalists may properly challenge carelessly presented numbers, challenge badly quantified cost-benefit analysis. They cannot ignore or decry economics as such. They cannot object to a recognition that the benefits of actions on behalf of the environment have a cost in foregone alternatives. Economics deals with choice, and environmentalists who push for a particular set of choices ought to think of themselves as applied economists.

I heard one dedicated environmentalist say, "Hopefully, we can have both conservation and growth." Such a statement does not recognize a conflict between conserving resources and using them to meet present-day human needs.

Yes, an environmentalist might concede, I recognize that people have to eat and want a dwelling to which they can come home. Yes, we do have to consider the costs, in forgone material wealth, of preservation. But what about the value of the vast natural world apart from mankind? Ought we not protect the natural order of things and limit the incursions in it of human beings, so that owls can nest, eagles can fly, and cougars roam?

THE PRESERVATION OF PRISTINE NATURE

The most dedicated environmentalist (not the extremist who spikes trees) assigns to Nature almost the status of a god. Nature, he implies, is above mankind. Nature has a design, a blueprint, and it issues warnings that people disregard at their peril.[7] Primordial nature, apart from men and women, is pure, pristine. People are not seen to be a part of nature. Men and women are intrusive, encroach upon nature, and contaminate it.

In this view, Nature has rights, or, at least animals and plants have rights ("species rights").

From the perspective of his critics, the environmentalist loves nature to excess. He loves green fields, forests, lakes, rivers, mountains, deserts, oceans; and no doubt he loves men and women, but he seems to care more for Nature than for people. Why? Because human beings change things around — erect houses, drill for water, channel streams, terrace hillsides, dam rivers, drain marshes, build cities.

Humans, he worries, upset the balance of nature, nature being the way things were in the absence of actions by men and women. To be sure, even without people, climate changes, old species disappear and new species come into existence. But environmentalists seem to believe that these nonhuman changes do not disrupt the balance of nature. Only when men and women move into an area, cultivate the land and harness the streams, is the natural order of things disturbed.

Critics of the environmentalists value human preferences and choices more highly. For them, people count for more and non-human species for less. Men and women have considerable, albeit not unlimited, control over nature, and it is right and proper that they exercise this power to better the lot of human beings.

Men and women can improve nature. Primitive peoples burned wood to heat their caves. Pioneers constructed log homes to keep out the wind and the rain. Farmers built fences to limit the depredations of mammals. They harnessed the wind with windmills and hoed the ground to minimize the encroachment of weeds. All through the ages, men have used the materials found in nature to achieve their goals — wood, water, air (oxygen), sand, copper, iron ore, hydrocarbons.

Individuals, through the institution of private property, exercise control over their immediate surroundings. *Communities* join together to construct dams and levees to confine and store water. With turbines, they capture and use the power of river currents. (To be sure, a sophisticated nonenvironmentalist recognizes that the forces of nature are powerful, that sometime human beings will be defeated in efforts to control natural forces, and that everyone must take into account the interdependencies in an ecosystem.)

Environmentalists do not like the idea of transportation, of moving things about. The shipment of commodities, they observe, changes the environment. When they find that water is short in their locality, environmentalists conclude that they have a crisis. But the world is full of water. And all through the ages men have transported water — on the back of camels, in aqueducts, in irrigation ditches, and nowadays by pipeline. Modern pumps have lowered the cost of transporting water across long distances. And when the costs of bringing in water are prohibitive, people import food and fiber from regions that have water in abundance. Regions lacking water bring in oranges from the irrigated San Joaquin Valley in California.

Frequently parochial, environmentalists, observing local scarcities, forget that products can be brought in from distant places; they leap to a conclusion of global short-ages. While sitting in a local traffic jam, surrounded by people in cars, they become Malthusians.

Environmentalists see the interdependencies in Nature (Nature, that is, apart from man) and they see that men frequently damage their natural surroundings. They do not recognize the pains that nature inflicts on man and fail to value human efforts to contain these pains. They fail to value the houses that men build to keep out the cold and protect families from dangerous animals, the irrigation systems that provide food, the dams that check devastating floods. They seem to say that people should just stay out of the way, or get out of the way, and let nature rule, let the floodwaters rage.

Dedicated environmentalists undervalue the human interdependencies that people create as they trade goods and services with one another. They do not like markets, nor do they recognize that people satisfy most of their wants through voluntary exchanges. They uncritically embrace the restrictive ties of community control.

Critics of environmentalists are concerned about jobs. They recognize that most people get a large part of their identities from their work and that unemployment is demoralizing. Particularly do critics of environmentalism worry about the poor, who cannot afford to worship Nature when they are cold and hungry.

Critics point out that the law of diminishing marginal utility applies to nature. As successive stands of old-growth forest are preserved, the consumer experiences less and less pleasure in their beauty.

As an economist who tries to avoid value judgments in his work, I cannot assert that concerns about the preferences of human beings are superior to concerns with the well-being of nonhuman species. I will, however, here speak as a noneconomist, and say something of my own preferences.

I am for balance. I do not think that men and women should set out to subdue nature, but neither do I believe that the natural environment should be placed off limits to human activities. I believe neither in a wilderness that must be tamed nor do I view nature as divine.

I look for a middle ground, for compromise. Meet nature halfway. Develop the land, but within constraints. Give freedom to individuals to change their surroundings, but have the community set reasonable limits. Set aside some land for the preservation of undisturbed nature — ancient forests, wild rivers, remote deserts. But always consider costs, the costs of using land and the costs of preserving nature.

One of the best discussions of this middle ground can be found in a book on gardening, *Second Nature: A Gardener's Education* by Michael Pollan.[8] Contending that people are a part of nature, he asserts that gardeners reshape nature, improve on it, create a "second nature." Pollan contends that people occasionally create ecosystems much richer than the ones they replace and he cites two examples, England's hedgerow landscape and the patchwork of fields and forests in present-day New England.

CHAPTER 3

THE LEGACY OF GOVERNOR McCALL

A charismatic Governor Tom McCall is given a lot of credit for Oregon's unique land law. He built a political career on voters' concern for the environment. However, he knew little about the economics of conservation. He believed that conservation is an absolute good.

Initially, Governor McCall focused on spillovers, most particularly on pollution in the Willamette River. He also saw the mess that occurred when people throw away bottles and cans. He pushed hard for a "Bottle Bill," the bill that enabled consumers to collect a deposit when they returned containers.

Later, Governor McCall switched his concerns from spillovers to preservation. He joined the battle to control the use of land. Local officials, he believed were too responsive to the pressures of developers and others interested in growth. Only the state, he believed, could hold these forces in check.[1] Governor McCall argued that he was not opposed to growth. He wanted planned growth, growth that was pollution free, measured, and prudent.[2]

Unfortunately, McCall's political skills were not matched by his understanding of economics. One of his supporters asserted that the Governor had little faith in the ideas of supply and demand, and didn't believe that the market system should work when it came to land. He thought land was too valuable for reliance on market forces.[3] (One might argue the opposite: Land is too valuable to ignore a market that records individual preferences on where to live and work.) When Governor McCall spoke of "growth addicts" he may not have understood the role of individual initiative in growth. He warned that opponents of land-use planning would use phrases like "freedom of choice," presumably without justification. Again and again he warned against "land speculators." [4]

McCall believed that the supply of critical resources was inelastic. He spoke in the language of the catastrophists: "Humanity has begun to exceed the earth's ability to provide." We are "using up the finite resources of this country . . . eating up tomorrow." We "might eventually find ourselves competing with the rats at the landfills for materials basic to economic survival." [5]

While Governor McCall wanted to preserve farm and forest land, he displayed no awareness that preservation has a cost. He did not recognize that the highest and best use of land might be in urban pursuits, that obstacles to the conversion of land from agriculture to urban activities stand in the way of economic development and a higher standard of living. He, like most conservationists, did not understand that failure to use a discount rate has an adverse influence on growth.

Curiously enough, late in his career, when he was being heckled for his support of nuclear energy, he screamed, "Damn it, I'm just telling you the tradeoffs." [6] Tragically, he did not recognize earlier that there is a tradeoff between preservation and development.

The Oregon land law that emerged in the 1970s reflects the environmental concerns of the time along with a fear of growth.

The pressures for development were very great. All around the state, developers wanted flat land and pushed for subdivisions. But flat land often was prime farm land. So growth was converting farm land to urban uses. "We do not want to become like Orange County in California," people were saying. "We do not want all of our land paved over for mall parking lots."

A major goal of Senate Bill 10, passed in 1969, was the preservation of prime farm lands. The bill required cities and counties to develop comprehensive plans and to zone all lands within their borders. In practice, however, enforcement of local plans was weak. County Commissioners encountered serious opposition, and often dragged their feet. People wanted to live in suburbs at the edge of cities. Developers wanted to accommodate these demands and were eager to buy farmland. Farmers ready to retire were willing to sell their land to developers.

After much struggle, the legislature passed Senate Bill 100 in 1973 and it was signed into law by the governor. The intention was to take heat off the county commissioners and transfer it to a state agency. The legislation created a Land Conservation and Development Commission (LCDC) that was to draft state planning Goals and Guidelines. Cities and counties and special districts were required to develop comprehensive plans that conformed to state goals.

Before the goals were issued, 28 community workshops were held around the state, to involve citizens in their preparation.

The legislature had attempted the impossible — state set goals and local implementation. Conflict between LCDC and local governments was inescapable. LCDC was to establish *standards* of land use in general terms. Counties and cities were to apply them in specific cases. Local governments, however, were reluctant to surrender their powers in matters of local interest. What if a county chose to implement the goals in a way not approved by LCDC?

In passing the legislation, the Senate issued a statement of intent. It asserted that the goals and guidelines were not to constitute zoning from the state level. The state was merely to set goals while the counties were to implement these goals. The impression was that land-use decisions would still be made by local agencies familiar with local conditions.

LCDC and DLCD (the administrative arm of LCDC), however, ended up with great powers.

A POWERFUL STATE

Based on its planning goals and planning guidelines, LCDC can and does issue regulations. In addition to the general guidelines for Goal Three, Agricultural Lands, LCDC has issued 13 pages of Oregon Administrative Rules (OAR 660-33-010 through 660-33-160).

LCDC/DLCD can and does review local comprehensive plans and land use ordinances for compliance with LCDC goals. Before it is adopted, LCDC must give prior approval to any legislative change by a local body. To be sure, the law did not explicitly state that LCDC could approve or disapprove local plans. To preserve the fiction that counties had not lost powers to the state, LCDC only "acknowledges" the plans that it approves. Use of the word "acknowledge" is dishonest. It suggests that LCDC merely takes note of local action. But it does more than this. It approves or disapproves. It exercises authority, throws its weight around. According to a leading land-use attorney, LCDC/DLCD is authorized to order a local government, special district, or state agency to comply in its plan, regulations, or decisions with LCDC goals and regulations.[7]

LCDC can require a change in the review process for local decisions. It can respond to a complaint by any citizen that alleges a pattern or practice in violation of state planning law, administrative rule, or local ordinance. It can insist that a local government eliminate the pattern and practice. It might tell a government that it has been issuing too many conditional use permits. LCDC can issue an enforcement order. Under an enforcement order, LCDC can impose nearly any type of oversight procedure that it wishes.

Under some circumstances, LCDC can review or perhaps even prohibit specific land-use decisions by a local government. It can prohibit such decisions until the local body completes (and has acknowledged) a comprehensive plan, or completes an amendment to its comprehensive plan, or completes a required periodic review of its comprehensive plan and land-use ordinances. Until the foregoing are completed, LCDC may review (or prohibit) annexations, subdivisions and other actions.

Local governments and the state jointly enforce the Urban Growth Boundary.[8] LCDC can approve or disapprove UGBs. Here is an example of LCDC/DLCD intervention:

In a letter to Debbie Times, Jackson County Planning Department (dated October 20, 1994), Melvin R. Lucas, Field Representative, Department of Land Conservation and Development (DLCD), wrote the following:

> Thank you for sending a copy of the latest proposed amendment to add about 68 acres to the Shady Cove Urban Growth Boundary (UGB).
>
> However, we still have concerns . . . We know Shady Cove is not developing at urban densities. We think this is mostly because the city does not have a municipal water system. Therefore, we feel the Shady

Cove UGB should not be expanded to enable the city to continue to develop at low densities on large parcels. . . . We recommend that this proposal be denied.

Please make this letter a part of the record of proceedings and notify us of the final decision . . .

Supporters of Oregon land law often assert that LCDC does no more than set goals and guidelines and that local governments make all concrete decisions with respect to land use. LCDC, it is said, is prohibited by law from making specific land management regulations, and only local governments enforce land-use regulations.[9] The reality is that LCDC, through DLCD, its administrative arm, is looking over the shoulder of a local jurisdiction when it acts. The Department of Land Conservation and Development sends letters to local bodies that express concerns about particular decisions. Two examples:

In a letter to Dick Converse, Jackson County Planning and Development (dated February 29, 1996), Ronald Eber, Rural Plan Analyst, Department of Land Conservation and Development (DLCD), wrote the following:

The department has had the opportunity to review the application for the Quail Point Golf Course at the Rogue Valley Manor dated December 29, 1995 (County File 96-1-CUP). The applicant requests a conditional use permit to build a nine hole golf course and a golf learning center in conjunction with an existing nine hole golf course at the Rogue Valley Manor. The golf learning center includes four practice holes, a driving range and three practice greens. Based on the information in the application, the department recommends that the county deny this application . . .

The proposal includes a tract (four tax lots) totalling 252 acres of which 47.82 acres are within the Medford

Urban Growth Boundary (UGB). Outside the Medford (UGB), the proposed site includes three tax lots that total 204.56 acres . . .

Jackson County cannot approve a conditional use permit for this application . . .

Please enter this letter into the record for this application. If any additional information is submitted in support of it, we request that the hearing be continued and the record remain open . . .

In a letter to Shirley Roberts, Jackson County Planning and Development Services (dated February 20, 1996), James W. Johnson, Farm/Forest Coordinator, Department of Land Conservation and Development (DLCD), wrote as follows:

The department has received notice of a request to establish a nonfarm dwelling on a 15.87 acre parcel (File 95-14-NF). The parcel is described as 35-2W-32, Tax Lot 2004 and is zoned Exclusive Farm Use (EFU). We have the following comments:

ORS 215.284(3)(b) and OAR 660-33-130(4)(c)(B) require findings that a proposed nonfarm dwelling be:

. . . situated upon a lot, or parcel or a portion of a lot or parcel, that is generally unsuitable for the production of farm crops and livestock or merchantable tree species, considering the terrain, adverse soil or land conditions, drainage and flooding, vegetation, location and size of tract.

OAR 660-33-130(4)(c)(B) further states:

A lot or parcel shall not be considered unsuitable solely because of size or location if it can reasonably be put to farm or forest use in conjunction with other land . . . A lot or parcel is presumed to be suitable if . . . in Western Oregon, it is composed predominately of Class I-IV soils. Just because a lot or parcel is unsuitable for one farm use does not mean it is not suitable for another farm use (emphasis added).

. . . Based upon the above-referenced comments, we recommend that this request be denied. We request that our letter and enclosures be entered into the record of the proceedings and that we receive a copy of the decision . . .[10]

No one could read the foregoing letters and conclude that LCDC/DLCD is not involved in site-specific land-use decisions. Attorneys and land-use consultants worry when they find letters like these in files, for they know that a local jurisdiction will take them seriously.

LCDC has the power of the purse. The state can withhold cigarette, liquor, and gas tax revenues from localities that fall behind in their planning.[11]

DISABLED LOCAL GOVERNMENTS

Within the limits of state land law and LCDC regulations, local jurisdictions have some room to maneuver. Much depends on local political forces. If the people in a locality favor growth and really want decisions to be made locally, county commissioners and city councils find that they have discretion. They can agree at least to small expansions of Urban Growth Boundaries, annexations, and subdivisions, and can resist the heavy hand of LCDC/DLCD. In Southern Oregon, Josephine, Douglas, and Klamath counties are in that category.

If, on the other hand, an active minority of people in the area are opposed to growth and care little for local option, the local authorities are limited in what they can do. When they decide in favor of a challenged expansion of the urban growth boundary or an annexation, the forces opposed to growth call in the powers of LCDC. After local authorities come under fire from LCDC/DLCD a few times, they get gun-shy and no longer attempt to get around LCDC's interpretation of state land law.

Jackson County is very reluctant to take on LCDC. And it has to cope with a painful reality. Back in the late 1970s, under pressure from LCDC to revise its comprehensive plan, it miszoned much of its land. Rather than look at soil maps to decide on what land should be classified Exclusive Farm Use (EFU), it simply looked at its tax rolls. It classified land as prime farm land that was assessment-district tax-deferred. This took care of the big farms. Then (in 1980) to satisfy people with just a few acres (owners of so-called hobby farms), it laid out EFU sign-up sheets. People on rocky hillsides signed up just to get the tax breaks.

Subsequently, all this misclassified land was locked into place with County ordinances and the difficult task of meeting LCDC criteria for nonfarm uses.

When Jackson County attempts to correct these past errors, it encounters the Jackson County Citizens League (JCCL), an affiliate of 1000 Friends of Oregon. These ideological environmentalists (many of whose members live in the City of Ashland) are vigorous and articulate opponents of growth. More interested in checking population increases in the County than in agricultural production, they oppose all changes that would allow development in rural areas. With JCCL ready to pounce on efforts to ameliorate inappropriate land-use constraints, Jackson

County, in land-use matters, is far more restrictive than neighboring Josephine, Douglas, and Klamath counties.

.   .   .

Now let us look more fully at the issues of farm and forest land protection.

CHAPTER 4

FARMLAND PROTECTION

In Oregon, the Land Conservation and Development Commission [LCDC] is expected to preserve farmland. Preservation, however, has a cost, a cost that is not taken into account in Oregon land law.

THE PRESERVATION OF FARMLAND

Environmentalists believe that urbanization threatens future supplies of food and fiber. We encounter these fears in the words of LCDC Goal 3 and its guidelines: *preserve and maintain agricultural lands* so as to meet existing and future needs for agricultural products; *minimize nonfarm uses* so as to allow for maximum agricultural productivity.

Goal 3 reflects the pessimism of environmentalists. Population growth, they believe, will cause future demand for food and fiber to be high. They assume that the carrying capacity of the land, the capacity of the land to feed and clothe the population is fixed (or, as a consequence of soil erosion, even declining). So, they conclude, we must minimize the nonfarm uses of land.

Environmentalists seldom consider the role of the market in an economy. They overlook the reality that when a growing demand for agricultural products exceeds the supply, prices rise, and then several things happen: The quantity of farmland increases. Idle farmland is brought into production. Unused land is fenced, fertilized, and cultivated. New farmland is developed. Forests are cleared, swamps are drained, dry land is irrigated, steep slopes are terraced, and roads are built into land that was previously inaccessible. An estimate of a few years ago was that "up to 260 million unused acres in the United States could be transformed into cropland, if farm prices justified the expense." [1]

In addition, when the price of farm products rises, existing farmland is used more intensively. Increased quantities of labor and capital are applied to land. Intensive agriculture is characteristic of densely populated regions. And finally, even as the demand for food and fiber rises, continuing research leads to more productive agricultural technology. Fallow land is cropped annually, machine power replaces animal power, chemical fertilizers are developed, seed is improved. A striking example is the "green revolution" of the late 1960s. Through use of high-yielding hybrids, chemical fertilizers, new crop strategies, and new harvesting methods, large increases in grain yields were achieved, particularly in India, Pakistan, and the Philippines.

In Chapter 13, we discuss what can best be described as the "myth" of a fixed carrying capacity.

Look at past history when the demand for food and fiber increased and technology changed. The forests in Europe were cut down, English marshes were drained, dikes were built to protect the coastal lowlands of the Netherlands. Hillsides were terraced throughout the world.

As heavy farm machinery came into existence, the hill farms of New England were abandoned and agricultural output expanded on large farms on flatland. With the development of the railroad and the steamship, the vast lands of North America were opened up and huge quantities of wheat were shipped to Europe.

Israel made the desert bloom. Drip irrigation, developed in Israel, made it possible to plant avocados on steep slopes on the West Coast of America.

But, say the environmentalists, all that is in the past. The future prospects for agriculture are grim.

DOOMSDAY: MALTHUSIAN ANXIETIES

Unless urban growth is constrained, assert the environmentalists, valuable farmland will be paved over for streets and parking lots. We or our heirs will go hungry, or at least people in the underdeveloped countries will starve.

Recall what we said in an earlier chapter: Preservationists, in their thinking, convert local shortages into global problems.

Pessimists worry about soil erosion and population growth. They argue that soils are being eroded away at a frightful rate. Lester Brown of World Watch asserts that 24 billion tons of soil are lost every year from erosion.[2] He is talking about a global loss of topsoil that could result in global food shortages.

It turns out, however, that much wind and water erosion simply shifts soil to a new location. Indeed, much of the world's food is grown on rich bottom lands and deltas formed by silt deposited downstream or by soil moved by the winds to new locations. One estimate is that 13 million tons of rich African soils are blown every year across the South Pacific to the Amazon forest floor.[3] To be sure, neither the figures that tell us how much soil is being lost to erosion or that tell us about quantities of soils redeposited should be taken seriously. First of all, absolute numbers are meaningless. They do not tell us how the figures of soil lost or gained compare with the total soil available for use. All they do is frighten us or reassure us. Secondly, such estimates are little more than guesses, resting, as they do, on a series of heroic assumptions that underlie shaky computer models.

Soil lost through erosion is replenished from the subsoil. Deep root penetration helps to convert subsoil to topsoil. The Soil Conservation Service of the U.S. Department of Agriculture calculates the rate at which this happens. Called the T-factor, the rate for deep soils is 1/30 of an inch per year.[4] Over a 30-year period, an inch of soil lost through erosion would be offset by the creation of new topsoil. "Crop production, says one soil scientist, "is as dependent on the subsoil as on the surface layer."[5]

Then we come to water, which, the pessimists tell us, is becoming dreadfully scarce. Water shortages, however, are decidedly local rather than world problems. Huge bodies of fresh water and vast numbers of running streams cover the land. All through the ages, men have transported water, on the backs of camels, in aqueducts, in irrigation ditches, and on trucks.

Reliance on distant water, to be sure, does present risks. Physical interruptions may occur, earthquakes or civil disorders. Economic, political, or legal factors may interrupt deliveries. Both farmers and city people have to live with risk. In Chapter 13, which deals with economic development, we point out that in any trading economy, people take risks of supply interruptions. Much of the world's population get vital foodstuffs from across the seas. Los Angeles gets water from the Owens Valley a couple of hundred miles away. A measure of risk and uncertainty is a necessary part of economic growth.

What about population? Is not population increasing so rapidly that we will not be able to feed people on existing and prospective farmland? Environmentalists tend to be Malthusians.

Malthus, in 1798, was the first pessimist who worried about population growth. He said that the production of food would grow arithmetically while population would grow geometrically. His forecast was wrong. Every child who is born has two hands as well as a mouth, and many have good brains as well. Malthus underestimated the future productivity of the hands of people who would be born, and he underestimated the brains of future scientists and engineers who would develop new agricultural technologies. He overestimated the number of mouths that would come into existence. He simply did not realize how difficult it is to forecast population. Demographers later came to recognize that it is particularly difficult to forecast fertility rates.

Curiously enough, Malthus is frequently cited as a person with immense foresight. Keep in mind that he forecast *global* overpopulation, not simply too many people in one place, like China or Rwanda. Yet, say the pessimists, because he will be proved right in the next decades or centuries, we must recognize his genius today. Malthus has been wrong for 200 years. How much longer will he have to be wrong before we might conclude that he was a failure as a demographer?

Sounder than global forecasts of overpopulation would be careful studies of local populations. Such studies might conclude that Egypt and parts of Mexico are overpopulated while Hong Kong, the Netherlands, and Oregon are not.

Nor is it clear that Oregon should protect its agricultural land so that it can help to feed the starving in Africa. When the United States ships its agricultural surpluses to Africa and Asia, it undermines indigenous agriculture and contributes to an international welfare dependency. The best way to help starving populations, assert some experts, is to give them money. Expenditures of such funds would attract supplies from nearby areas and strengthen trade ties. Trade has done much to eliminate famine from the world. (The United States might still want to encourage birth control in poor areas with dense populations so as to reduce the pressure on fragile democratic governments.)

Then, with no support in facts or analysis, environmentalists forecast *sudden* change, and, of course, change for the worse. Soil erosion, population growth, water shortages, all of these changes suddenly will come to a head. Catastrophe. Doomsday.

Environmentalists do not care to recognize that global difficulties in agriculture would appear gradually and that small price increases would stimulate changes necessary to overcome the difficulties. Perhaps the most striking belief is that we can no longer expect improvements in agricultural technology to increase food production. All of a sudden, technological change is to cease.

The main reason to feel optimistic about the future, however, is the unlikelihood of a sudden global change. There is no reason to expect world-wide catastrophe. If population and agricultural prices rise, unused but accessible lands will come into cultivation. Farmers will use land more efficiently, everyone will use water more carefully, waste of all sorts will decline, people will adjust to change. Technological change will increase the alternatives open to men and women.

In the 1990s, we are looking at genetic engineering and "precision agriculture." From biogenetics, we can expect disease resistant genes that boost plants' natural immunity and a super rice that in a decade will triple yields. Satellite technology is being used on some farms for precise applications of fertilizers and pesticides. With knowledge obtained through use of computers and the satellite Global Positioning System, a farmer can apply different quantities of fertilizer and pesticides to each particular location within a large field.

Stagnation theses have a long history. Again and again in the past people have decided that everything has been invented. In the 1930s and 1940s, Keynesian economists decided that we could expect little innovation in the future. They thought that recent developments in transportation, communication, and power had exhausted the possibilities. Subsequently, of course, we experienced striking technological changes — jet aircraft, fuel efficient automobiles, television, nuclear power, space travel, a green revolution in agriculture.

The pessimists predict doomsday, but they give no reasons why difficulties will not emerge gradually and give us time to adjust. It is ironic that even as the pessimists talk about the catastrophic loss of farmland, elected officials in most of the developed world are struggling to deal with agricultural surpluses.

PLAY IT SAFE

Still, argue the determined environmentalist, we cannot afford to risk losing farmland. Decades from now, people may starve if we cover the land with factories, shopping centers, parking lots, streets, and houses. We must conserve farmland just in case.

This is extreme risk aversion, and it has a cost. The cost is forgone economic development, forgone manufactured goods, commerce, finance, services, and housing, perhaps even forgone research in agricultural productivity. When the law keeps land in uneconomic farm activities, people in the future will live less well than if government were to step aside and allow farmland owners to sell the land for urban pursuits.

IRREVERSIBLE DECISIONS

The preservationists argue that we cannot reverse decisions to construct buildings and pave over the land. Some actions, however, can be reversed. In times of war, nations find use for every inch of idle land. They tear out lawns and sow vegetables. They put back into production lands set aside for conservation reserves. To be sure, the costs of many reversals are prohibitive. But communities do have other alternatives. They can and do look outside for food and fiber previously grown locally. They can ship in food and fiber. People at a distance open up new agricultural lands. Men use existing farmland more intensively.

THE ROLE OF WATER IN THE PROTECTION OF FARMLAND

For not very good reasons, land law in many parts of the United States is drawn up to preserve agricultural land. Few people know that the prices set on irrigation water around the country also serve to protect agriculture. Farmers almost everywhere get irrigated water at a price that is far below the cost of delivery. In the Westlands Water District of California, irrigators pay $8.00 to $31.00 per acre foot for water that costs from $61.00 to $80.00. Cities bid up to $200.00 per acre foot for water rights.[6] The World Bank recognizes the anomaly. It points out that water, in most countries, is usually delivered by the state, at prices far below real costs. The Bank now is calling for proper water pricing and the development of water markets like those in the U.S. West, where farmers sell their water rights to cities.[7]

Were farmers charged the full price for their irrigation water, they would in many cases not continue in agriculture. It is not surprising that proposals to charge the full price for water is political dynamite.

But suppose we focus on efficiency in rural and urban economies. Consider a system in which government agencies priced water as a commodity (with, to be sure, regulatory commissions to prevent the imposition of monopoly prices). The consequences would be striking. Many farmers would leave farming. Cities would buy and use the water that was released from agriculture.

Were decisions on land-use as well as decisions on water consumption made in markets, the employment of land would reflect the demand for land in both its rural and urban uses. The delivery of water would reflect the costs of delivery and the demands, urban and rural, for water. Land near cities would be transferred from rural to urban uses. Water previously used to irrigate farms would be purchased for municipal and industrial users, and food and fiber previously grown locally would be shipped from distant parts.

AGRICULTURE IN THE ROGUE VALLEY

Jackson and Josephine Counties are required by state law to preserve farmland: they may not allow it to be converted to urban uses. The problem is that agriculture in the Valley is in serious trouble. Farmers are barely breaking even or are losing money. They do not know where to turn to find a way out of their dilemma. They cannot make it in agriculture, and they are not allowed to sell their land for non-agricultural uses.

In Chapter 3, I reported how poor land in Jackson County was misclassified as high-quality farmland and how efforts to classify this land more appropriately have been defeated.

Consider pear orchards. A decade ago, the orchardists

of Jackson and Josephine Counties had found a wonderful niche market for themselves, in specialty pears (Bosc, Red pears, Seckels, and so forth). Now they face domestic and foreign overproduction, and other regions have a comparative advantage in these highly competitive markets. (The best account of pear orchards in the region is in a paper by Mike Naumes, President of Naumes, Inc., "The Future of Agriculture in Jackson County." It was delivered to the Medford Chamber of Commerce on April 17, 1995.[8])

Consumers want (and supermarket buyers demand) large pears. Rogue Valley soils, however, are poor, suitable only for small fruit. Small fruit can only be sold at low prices. In addition, competition in specialty pears is keeping sale prices down, competition coming from fruit produced in the states of Washington and California and in the Southern Hemisphere (especially Chile).

Costs of pear production are up: Packing costs have increased (the costs of boxes, pear wrap, and so forth). The cost of stickering each fruit with a Price Lookup Code (demanded by supermarket buyers) is prohibitive. (To sticker fruit, packers would have to construct entirely new packing lines, even as they are losing money on the old lines). Critical fungicides used to fight decay have been outlawed, so the producer often has to repack boxes of decayed fruit, adding to costs of production. Because of their unfavorable location, orchardists in the Rogue Valley have to absorb high shipping costs to reach and compete in distant markets.

Defenders of farmland protection advise orchardists to shift to other crops, but the alternatives are almost as bleak. Apples, nectarines, peaches, plums, cherries, melons, and grapes all are coming in from the Southern Hemisphere and holding down prices in the Rogue Valley. The Valley lacks processing plants for sweet corn and tomatoes. It lacks big feedlots for beef cattle. Hogs can be fed cheaper on field corn in the Midwest. Receipts from field crops at best allow the farmer to break even, leaving him no return on his labor and capital.

Banks in the Rogue Valley are increasingly reluctant to lend; credit lines are threatened. When they do lend, banks insist on higher interest rates to cover what they perceive to be higher risks.

Many observers expect that the banks or county governments will end up owners of the land in the Rogue Valley, when farmers can no longer service their loans and pay their taxes.

But let us suppose that things begin soon to look a little better, and that many if not most farmers can begin to make modest profits. The return on farmland still is likely to be less than the return on this land if changed to urban uses. The market price of lands at the periphery of cities indicates that the highest and best use of this land is in manufacturing, commerce, finance, or housing for urban workers. Restrictions in its conversion to urban uses slows the rate of growth and deprives people of the goods and services that they want.

We have already considered the role of water in agriculture. Over time agriculture will become a much smaller part of the Rogue Valley economy. A proper price on irrigation water would hasten this development. Land and water in the Valley would be shifted from low-valued agricultural pursuits to urban activities for which the demand is greater. The Rogue Valley would import more of its food from the Willamette Valley in the north, California in the south, and farms to the east.

RURAL CULTURE

Some might argue that uneconomic agriculture should be preserved in order to preserve rural culture, preserve the values of attachment to the earth, hard work, and family life. It is, however, the small family farm, not the large commercial farm, that is the repository of traditional rural values. And yet Oregon land-use regulations discriminate against small farms.

THE INCREDIBLE BIAS AGAINST SMALL-SCALE AGRICULTURE

If the goal of Oregon land law is delivery of produce to city people at reasonable prices, the administrative rules adopted by the Land Conservation and Development Commission (LCDC) are strikingly deficient.

The rules assume, incredibly, that only large commercial farms are efficient. LCDC rules look only at physical size and gross income in determination of efficiency. The costs of farming are ignored.

In Oregon, for rural land not designated as rangeland, the law requires that a new parcel be not smaller than 80 acres. For rangeland, the legal minimum is 160 acres. Individuals cannot build a house on low-value farmland that yields a gross annual income from sale of farm products of less that $40,000. A person cannot build a house on high-value farmland that yields a gross annual income of less than $80,000. In the administrative rules adopted by LCDC, size of parcel and gross farm income are the measures of efficiency. LCDC does not consider cost. Ostensibly, these rules are to preserve efficient commercial farming and protect the supply of food and fiber. Actually, they stand in the way of efficient, small-scale agriculture and prevent people from choosing life on small acreage at the edge of a city.

Engineering efficiency compares physical inputs with physical outputs. Economic efficiency compares expenditures with receipts, or, when money prices are not available, compares non-monetary costs with benefits. LCDC simply uses acreage and gross receipts as a measure of efficiency. A farm with 80 acres of land and gross receipts of $80,000 is declared to be efficient. Smaller farms are presumed to be inefficient. Land may not be divided into small units. Dwellings may not be built on small parcels.

Economists look at efficiency in a more sophisticated way. In a competitive market with no spillovers, profit is a good measure of efficiency. A 20-acre farm with receipts of $15,000 and costs of $13,000 would be efficient. An 80-acre farm with receipts of $85,000 and costs of $125,000 would be inefficient. Consideration of size alone is not enough to determine efficiency.

The costs of family labor and the necessary profits of a part-time farmer are low. The family loves the semi-rural life. Even with a low return on labor, it still chooses to work in the countryside. And, the part-time farmer with a job in town, requires only a small premium for risk. In a drought year, he can live on his wages. The life of the part-time farmer is a good one. He works in town, as a janitor, roofer, or the like. Then he comes home to more satisfying pursuits. (He is not only the affluent professional who operates a hobby farm.)

Sowed, cultivated, and harvested by low-cost labor and by part-time farmers who require only a small premium for risk, produce from small-scale agriculture is delivered to the community at low cost.

Environmentalists who seek to preserve farmland as open space coalesce with commercial farmers who dislike the encroachment of city people in the countryside and, perhaps, do not want the competition of small-scale farmers for the land that they purchase at a low price or rent cheaply. Together environmentalists and commercial farmers oppose what they call non-farm dwellings. Commercial farmers find that edge-of-city people criticize their spraying of pesticides, object to dust, and sometimes harbor vandals who break down fences or damage crops with off-road vehicles. A coalition emerges, a coalition of environmentalists who do not want to see buildings in the countryside and big commercial farmers who do not want to operate near refugees from the city. The two groups together have engaged in relentless efforts to prohibit dwellings in the countryside.

Those who want to prohibit small-scale agriculture fail to consider alternative ways of dealing with spillover conflict between farmers and the people who dwell at the edge of cities. They fail to consider buffer zones, right-to-farm laws, effective law enforcement against vandalism, and so forth. It seems easier to deprive households of choice than to reconcile conflicting interests.

To be sure, some gains and losses cannot be measured in monetary terms. Then economists, and the rare economically oriented environmentalists, use cost-benefit analysis. Efforts are made to measure non-monetary benefits and costs. What is the value of a wildlife habitat? What is the cost (the disutility) of toxic runoff into streams?

There is no reason to believe that a comprehensive cost-benefit analysis would show small-scale agriculture to be less efficient than large commercial agriculture. Small farmers might be more concerned to protect wildlife habitat than large commercial farmers. They might use less fertilizer and might be less responsible for non-point pollution than commercial operators.

LCDC seems not to be aware of the important role that small-scale agriculture plays in Oregon and America. Seventy-three percent of the nation's farms are classified by the Economic Research Service of the United States Department of Agriculture as small farms, defined as units with annual gross farm sales of less the $50,000. These units farm 32 percent of the acreage and account for 12 percent of farm sales. "Thus," according to the retired publisher of the Capital Press, "a large majority of farms in the United States must depend on outside income if they are family farm operations."[9] The American Farmland Trust, which is genuinely devoted to the conservation of farmland nationwide, published a report in 1986, "Small Is Beautiful: The Importance of Small Farms in America."[10] It contended that in 1982, eighty-one percent of Oregon farms were small, defining small as less than $40,000 in annual gross sales of agricultural products.

Looking at LCDC rules, I find it difficult to believe that the agency is serious about agricultural efficiency and the delivery of food and fiber to consumers. Senseless measures of efficiency and strong opposition to semi-rural dwellings point to a different goal, the protection of open space, the desire for a countryside with few people and buildings. To be sure, what I write here suggests that people devoted to the environment are insincere and do not really care about farm efficiency or consumer welfare. Or, at the least, that they lack insight into their own motives. I hesitate to pursue this line of inquiry.

But consider the following: Suppose LCDC and its supporters were interested solely in preserving open space, and could not care less about farm efficiency and consumer welfare. What would the agency put forth as land-use regulations? How about 80 and 160 acre minimums and gross income minimums of $40,000 and $80,000 as a requirement for the construction of rural dwellings? When I think along such lines, I wonder if keeping people out of the countryside is not really what Oregon land-use regulation is all about.

I deal with this subject of *exclusion* in land-use law in Chapter 11.

CHAPTER 5

PROTECTION OF FOREST LANDS

The forest goals of the Land Conservation and Development Commission (LCDC), stated in Goal 4, are to preserve forest lands and protect the state's forest economy. These objectives are to be achieved through economically efficient forest practices. The continuous growing and harvesting of forest tree species is to be the leading use of forest land.

Goal 4 also requires that forest operations meet standards of soil and water conservation. There are, however, spillovers into neighboring activities when companies cut trees.

SPILLOVERS IN FORESTRY

The harvest of timber may contribute to soil erosion. When soil washes into streams, it adversely affects fish and hurts downstream fishermen. Heavy equipment, used in the harvest of timber, compacts the soil. Run-off fails to replenish groundwater and may cause floods, so people who rely on wellwater may be hurt as well as those who are flooded out. Here we have fairly clear cases of market failure, although timber people contend that the adverse consequences of erosion and compaction are exaggerated.

What about a loss of viewscapes, changed views as a consequence of a tree harvest? Is this a case of market failure, and a situation in which the community might properly intervene?

A timber company proposes to clearcut a forest, and replace it with seedling trees. People object. Neighbors and regular passersby argue that they will lose a beautiful view. For a long time, they contend, the site will be an eyesore.

Perhaps the company should be considerate of its neighbors and eschew a timber harvest, or at least leave a buffer of trees along the road or on the edge of its land. Ought the community insist that the company forgo large profits on its behalf? Defenders of property rights contend that the community should compensate a company if it expects it to forgo large profits or spend large sums to preserve a view. Such a contention raises the "takings" issue, which I deal with in Chapter 14.

Even as we recognize spillovers as market failure, we have to admit the existence of gray areas. Just how considerate of its neighbors should an enterprise be? Advocates of limited government might hope for a lot of neighborly consideration, so as to minimize the role of government, and then judges with the wisdom of Solomon to settle civil disputes.

When there are clear-cut cases of market failure, of indefensible spillovers, the case for governmental intervention is strong. When timber companies, looking only at short-term profit and loss statements, do not meet the justified concerns of their neighbors, they can expect them to look to legislatures and courts for protection.

Apart from spillovers, however, timber markets do a good job of serving consumers and producers of wood products.

CONSERVATION AND TIMBER PRODUCTION

The demand for logs is a derived demand, derived from the demand for construction materials, utility poles, paper, furniture, and other products. The supply of timber is a function of the costs of producing, cutting, and hauling trees. The costs of harvest vary for clearcutting, selective logging, thinning, and salvage logging. There are, most decidedly, economies of large-scale production in timber harvesting. Costs decline as the area harvested is larger and as the number of board feet cut is greater. One large company I contacted will not consider logging an area smaller than 40 acres.

Critics of capitalism are surprised to learn that timber companies conserve both trees and forests. They seem to think that only government is concerned with conservation. Forest enterprises conserve trees by caring for them over the years until the time is right for harvest. (They preserve forests when they harvest the trees and plant new seedlings.) Company acts of conservation provide timber for future use. The costs of conservation, however, are high, and firms properly take them into account. When harvest is postponed, timber may have to be thinned. Resources may have to be used to control insects and disease and to protect against or fight fire. Holding timber is risky — the physical risks of fire, the market risk of a decline in prices, the regulatory risk of new rules that increase the costs of forest management.

Environmentalists are skeptical of markets. They do not like the idea that decisions with regard to forest growth and harvests are subject to market considerations. They doubt that the market properly values forests and forest products. They shudder to think that something as mundane as timber prices, costs of conserving forests, and profit should determine when trees should be cut.

FEARS OF A TIMBER FAMINE

Conservationists and government officials often succumb to anxieties about future shortages. In 1911, early-day conservationists raised the specter of a timber famine. Most particularly, people talked about a "hickory problem." A lot of hickory was being used for railroad ties and bridgeplanks. Many people feared that hickory as a resource, for which there was believed to be no substitute, was being seriously depleted. Forty years later, however, because of a decline in the demand for hickory, the Forest Service had new fears. It worried that hickory was taking over the Eastern hardwood forests and it urged the railroads to use more hickory.[1]

Malthusian-like fears that we will run out of timber fail to consider the possibilities of technological change. As stumpage values rise, enterprises learn how to get more raw material out of forests and more products out of logs brought into the mill. Plywood from peeled veneers uses wood more effectively than lumber produced with saws. Plywood peelers peel logs down to four or five inches in diameter and the remainder of a log is converted into 2 × 4s, particle board, or chips for pulp and paper. Smaller trees can be used for a wide range of products. Low-grade trees can be used in the manufacture of wafer board, which is a substitute for lumber and plywood. Sawdust is used for fuel in dryers and other equipment requiring heat.

New technologies in the future will enable enterprises that manufacture wood products to economize further in the use of·timber.

PRESERVATION OF FOREST LANDS

What can be said for the role of government in the protection of forests and forest lands? The case for a governmentally-mandated guardianship, as opposed to a market-oriented preservation, is weak. Yet LCDC protects forest land as a matter of course. It limits the conversion of forest land to alternative rural or urban uses.

In many cases, the value of land in alternative pursuits exceeds its value as timberland. Consumers may prefer homesites, a destination resort, a dude ranch, or the products of urban manufacture. Businessmen may want to purchase timberland and develop it for recreation, manufacturing, commerce, or finance. They believe that consumers want the products of investment in these activities.

When the law prohibits the sale of forest lands to people who recognize its value in alternative activities, it lowers the rate of economic development. Consumers are denied desired vacations in the countryside, desired urban goods and services, or denied urban housing that they would like. Preferred structures cannot be built and capital goods that would serve the future cannot be manufactured.

Preservationists, however, do not accept market valuations of alternative land uses.

To defend their positions, preservationists have to argue that government officials, as representatives of the community, can better value future goods and services than can private individuals. They have to argue that individuals are short-sighted.

Not only must preservation decisions reflect careful evaluations of future benefits and costs, they must *discount* future outcomes.

Preservationists and conservationists are seldom aware of the interest rate, the discount rate, and its important role in the allocation, through time, of scarce resources. Officials and planners need to recognize the power of compound interest and how it impacts decisions to conserve resources.

In this chapter, we look at the cost of waiting, of foregoing early gains.

DISCOUNT RATES AND THE COST OF TIMBER CONSERVATION

Timber companies discount late returns because of the lapse of time from planting to harvest. Consider the following two examples:

Example 1: Decision of a Private Enterprise

A timber company is considering a possible 40-year wait before it harvests a particular stand of forest. It forecasts receipts of $1,200 (in present prices) for the sale of the timber and expenditures of $200 for cutting and hauling the logs. So net income for the timber would be $1,000. The company forecasts a real interest rate of 5 percent. (A real rate is one that is corrected for inflation.) The present value of the $1,000 that it would net for the harvest is $142.05.

$$V_o = \frac{1,000}{(1.05)^{40}} = 142.05$$

where V_o is present value and reflects 40 years of compound discount.*

---

*
$$V_o = \frac{V_f}{(1+i)^n}$$

where V_o is present value

V_f is future value

i the real interest rate in hundreths, and

n the number of years.

Example 2: Decision of a Government Agency

Government agencies often have longer time horizons than private companies. If the timber is federally owned, the Bureau of Land Management might plan to wait 100 years before it sells the timber for harvest. Suppose it forecasts the same $1,200 in receipts and $200 in expenditures and forecasts the same real interest rate. The present value of the $1,000 net income realized when the logs are sold would be $7.60.

$$V_0 = \frac{1,000}{(1.05)^{100}} = 7.60$$

By planning to hold on to the timber much longer (for 100 years instead of 40), the Bureau would expect a dramatically smaller value than the timber company ($7.60 as compared with $142.05).

What do these figure mean? With present values so low, the decision to conserve timber for a long time has to be looked at carefully. Moreover, the values in these examples overstate the income that would be obtained over the life of the trees. The examples include no costs for years of preservation — thinning, spraying for insecticides, fire protection, and so forth.

On the basis of the figures provided in the two examples, it looks like good stewardship would call for a harvest in 40 years. The present value of such a cut is positive and substantially greater than the return on a harvest delayed for 100 years.

Forests harvested early provide wood for buildings or furniture or paper at an earlier date. Consumers do not have to wait so long for lower prices. Businessmen earlier experience lower prices for wood products used in the formation of capital — perhaps 2×8s used in the construction of buildings.

In these examples, I have assumed that the land remains in forests. However, a higher rate of return might call for employment of the land in totally different uses, alternative rural uses or urban uses. Were the land transferred to recreational use, vacationers might experience lower prices in destination resorts or dude ranches. If the trees were removed and the land converted to urban uses, consumers might find lower prices on the products of the city. Factories, workshops, commercial buildings, or housing might be the best use of the land. The community might prefer that the land be used for affordable housing.

Use of a discount rate maximizes the rate of growth in an economy. Growth not only provides resources for private consumption goods and services and for private investment, it also increases the tax base and provides resources for public goods and services — highways, bridges, schools, bicycle paths, parks, environmental cleanup, social services, and so forth.

Conversely, failure to use a discount rate in decisions to harvest timber or decisions to keep land in forestry checks the rate of growth in an economy. Once again, compound interest (discount) is powerful. Only when we look at the power of compound interest can we see how much is lost when enterprises or governments fail to employ a discount rate in the allocation of scarce resources.

When governments do fail to employ a discount rate in considering alternative uses for land, or when they fail to insist that others do so, they check growth in the economy. They stand in the way of improvements in the standard of living of their populations.

Although, the word "development" is in its title, the Land Conservation and Development Commission does not recognize the role of the interest rate in matters of economic development. Implicit in the goals and guidelines of LCDC is a zero rate of discount. That is, LCDC believes that a 2×8 wood joist one year from now is equal in value to a 2×8 on hand immediately, even though it is not available as capital for the next 365 days, not available, say, to support a floor in a new machine shop. The 2×8 does not contribute to growth during the coming year, so the economy grows more slowly than it would if a contractor could obtain the lumber right away.

Let us see how an interest rate might be employed if LCDC understood and recognized the significance of the discount rate. A developer appears before a local planning commissions and asks for an expansion of the Urban Growth Boundary. He provides figures to show that demand for housing would make it profitable for him to develop a new subdivision. Commissioners, properly briefed by a sophisticated LCDC, ask him what discount rate he used in his calculations. He replies that he used a combination of medium and long-term rates, reflecting the periods his capital will be tied up during the various phases of the project.

Opponents of this development contend that the land should be left in forestry (or farming). Commissioners ask these people for their forecasts of the prices of timber products and costs of production. (An insistence that opponents of development actually attempt careful economic forecasts in lieu of simple emotive language predicting doomsday would be refreshing.) After the advocates of farmland protection put forth, no doubt reluctantly, their forecasts of farm prices and costs, the Commissioners ask, "And what discount rate did you use in your calculations?"

If the opponents of change advocate a low or zero "social" rate of discount, the Commissioners ask them to justify not using a market rate that reflects individual preferences for present and future goods and services.

The market rate of interest, environmentalists might say, reflects the preference of individuals, impatient individuals, people who really should postpone gratification. If individuals choose not to wait, they would argue, the community must override these short-sighted preferences. At this point, a thoughtful Commission might challenge an elitist view that ordinary people who participate in the market are short-sighted and inadequately concerned with the future. Commissioners might also point out that use of a discount rate does not depend on impatient consumers. All it requires is that economic growth is an objective, that the availability of resources for early reinvestment is desirable.

Were LCDC to require that the interest rate be considered in matters of land conservation, it would be recognizing that there is a trade-off between conservation and growth. It would be recognizing that an insistence on conservation without regard to consequences acts to check growth.

In a revision of its Goal 2: Land Use Planning, LCDC could state, "Both private parties and public agencies should explicitly employ a discount rate in proposals for alternative uses of land." It might add, "If a lower than market rate of discount is used, a 'social' rate of discount, it should be justified by a clear statement of why community time preferences should override the preferences of individuals."

Perhaps we can dream of a day when a sophisticated electorate insists that consideration of a proper discount rate is part of all hearings on governmentally mandated conservation. Indeed, when voters become fully aware of the costs of conservation, they may vote for representatives who will change Oregon land law.

In Goal 4, LCDC requires forest practices to be consistent with sound management of soil, air, water, fish, and wildlife resources. We will look at the issues involved in the protection of entire ecosystems.

ECOSYSTEMS

An ecosystem is a set of organisms and their physical environment, with the organisms interacting with one another and their surroundings. A system that is sustainable would be one that supplies the same goods and services over a period of time. What is sustained might simply be surroundings that people look at or a piece of nature that people value just because it is there — a viewscape, a scenic waterway, a tree-lined hiking trail, or an old-growth forest. (No one who thinks about sustainable ecosystems would think about an old-growth forest that is changeless. But people may value an old-growth forest that is left alone by men and women and that changes only as a consequence of non-human forces — winds, rain, sun, and fire.)

More interesting than ecosystems totally free of human involvement are systems that include people, like an "eco-field" of domestic crops or an "eco-forest" that is periodically harvested. Such systems would not be totally changeless, of course, but would be systems that returned to a particular state of existence at specified intervals. An ecosystem that included human activities might be a farm that every spring would have soil fertility appropriate for a particular set of crops, along with particular wildlife. Or it might be a forest that every 40 years would have a specified number of board feet of standing timber ready to harvest, along with particular, trees, wildlife species, rotting timber on the ground, bacteria, fungi, and so forth.

Some individual or body would have to set the physical boundaries of the ecosystem — a particular 160-acre farm, a particular national park, a bounded 4,000-acre second-growth forest.

A beginning date would have to be specified.

A person or a group of people would have to be selected to designate the components of the system. The components of a sustainable farm might be soil suitable for winter wheat, specified trees at the fenceline, particular shrubs as cover for wildlife, particular bird and animal wildlife, and so forth. The components of sustainable forest might be particular tree species, mammals and birds, specified snags and fallen timber on the ground, particular bacteria, fungi, specified roads, and so forth.

Here is where the subject really gets interesting. Who decides? Whose preferences count?

A dedicated environmentalist would minimize human preferences and human intervention. Nature is and should be species rich? Nature should dominate. Environmentalists want large boundaries around protected ecosystems. Many environmentalists want to preserve grizzly bears, cougars and wolves, though they kill domesticated livestock and an occasional human child or adult. In India man-eating tigers are protected; in Africa, elephants that trample the crops of poor farmers. Preservationists often are unhappy with changes brought about by men and women. They oppose monocultures, tree farms or game farms. They do not like human artifacts (houses, vehicles, roads, and so forth) and they do what they can to confine people to compact cities.

Environmentalists, moderate or extreme, usually are part of the liberal-left. They are skeptical of markets and private property. When they do recognize human preferences, they focus on collective preferences, preferences of the community that are implemented by government.

Critics of environmentalists see things differently. They assign a much larger role to individual preferences, as opposed to community preferences. They believe that job and consumption needs of autonomous households are important. The desires of individuals to fell timber, convert it into lumber, market it, and buy it for the construction of houses are considered at least as important as the preservation of habitat for endangered species. The needs of people who receive help from government social programs are weighted high compared to the preferences of those who want action to preserve resources. In Jackson County, Oregon those concerned with the plight of the poor want a harvest of trees that generates revenue for county-financed assistance to the impoverished. They consider such programs more important than the preservation of the habitat of the spotted owl.

Non-environmentalists recognize that people can exercise a considerable control over nature. They can build houses to keep out the wind and the rain, construct dams and levees to confine and store water, hunt to limit the depredations of mammals and birds, spray chemicals to minimize the adverse consequences of insects and weeds.

To be sure, a sophisticated non-environmentalist does recognize that the forces of nature are powerful, that sometime human beings will be defeated in efforts to control nature, and that everyone must take into account the interdependencies in an ecosystem.

A sophisticated advocate of the market is not uncritical of capitalism. He recognizes that, along with useful trading opportunities, there are undesirable spillovers in market economy. He understands both the good and the bad features of capitalism.

Economists seem to be better at recognizing unfortunate interdependencies in an economic system than ecologists are at recognizing unsatisfactory interdependencies in an ecosystem. Some natural forces are inimical to human beings. Warm temperatures and early snow melts cause floods that kill people and domestic animals. Stagnant water is the breeding place for mosquitoes that spread disease amongst a variety of mammals. Wild animals kill livestock and people. Nature is not always benign; sometimes it can properly be identified as an enemy of mankind.

Critics of environmentalists, people concerned for individual and family welfare, may be willing to accept the preservation of small, clearly-bounded ecosystems — with, to be sure, people being part of the systems. Our less-used national parks might meet these standards. (In Chapter 2, I dealt with the costs of preserving completely pristine natural environments.)

Let me say it once again. Environmentalists are on the right track in forestry when they look at spillovers (like soil erosion, damage to streams, and perhaps changes in viewscapes). They fail when they advocate the preservation of woodlands without a careful analysis of the costs of such actions.

Still, controversy rages. Save the forests, protect farmland, preserve greenspace. Or, alternatively, free up land for development.

. . .

In the following chapters, I will look at five models of land use in and around cities: historical sprawl, flexible urban growth boundaries, the rigidly compact city, greenbelts with satellite communities, and what I shall call orderly sprawl.

CHAPTER 6

HISTORICAL SPRAWL

In the early days, cities in America just grew. People spread out at the edge of a city, on large lots and small acreage. Farmers sold off pieces of land to individuals who chose to live at the edge of the city. Or they sold their farms to contractors who built for sale. Some houses constructed on the edge of the city were large, attractive, and expensive. Others were small and cheap. Some inhabitants relied on septic tanks. Others had only privies. Residents walked or drove on gravel roads, with drainage ditches at the sides. Empty lots were scattered about. It was a free-for-all.

The problem was that individuals who had moved to the periphery for privacy and solitude found intrusive neighbors moving in around them. The more affluent and far-sighted bought large parcels for protection, but the less well-off did not have this alternative. They could respond with anger to the incursions of newcomers, or they could, like the pioneers of old, move on when they began to see their neighbors' smoke. But people are reluctant to relocate and moving is expensive.

Old timers, the people who came early, sometimes tried to organize in order to keep out newcomers, perhaps tried to get zoning restrictions which would keep new people from building nearby. But early settlers often were individualists, conservatives, believers in private property, not communitarians. While they raged against newcomers, they often did not get along well with one another.

Enter the affluent who have chosen life on the periphery, prosperous retirees or families with two cars, children, and a riding lawnmower. These sturdy members of the middle class get together to stop the influx, stop people from coming in and doing what they did. And they make common cause with the environmentalists, who challenge "sprawl," which, they say, is wasteful of land, and wasteful of resources used in sewers, streets, and other infrastructure.

. . .

In place of an unruly and sprawled out city, environmentalists, with cheering sections in the suburbs, advocate the compact city — efficient (so they say), well-regulated, and disciplined. But cities continue to spread out.

CHAPTER 7

FLEXIBLE URBAN GROWTH BOUNDARIES

The Land Conservation and Development Commission (LCDC) defines open space broadly. Open space consists of lands used for agriculture or forests, along with wetlands, beaches, tidal marshes, scenic resources, wildlife preserves, nature reservations or sanctuaries, and public and private golf courses. What do all these kinds of open space have in common? They are lands with few or no people and few or no human artifacts, few buildings, vehicles, and other evidences of human life. Land preservationists do not want people to be scattered out on the earth's surface. People mostly should live together, in compact cities.

LCDC, however, has had only limited success in its efforts to get people to live in tight clusters.

IRRESISTIBLE SPRAWL

Early in the 1990s, the Department of Land Conservation and Development (DLCD), the administrative arm of LCDC, commissioned ECO Northwest to study recent development patterns inside and outside Urban Growth Boundaries (UGBs). ECO Northwest studied four metro-

71

politan areas (Portland, Medford, Bend, and Brookings). It found that all of these areas developed land inside UGBs at densities lower than planned and developed land outside UGBs at densities higher than planned. All four metropolitan areas placed single-family houses in multiple-family zones.[1] In each of the areas studied, residential development resulted in low-density housing outside and around most or all of the UGBs.[2]

A U.S. Department of Agriculture report shows that in Oregon, between 1982 and 1992, a large amount of land was converted from resource land to residential development, 240 square miles in the Willamette Valley alone, an area almost twice the size of Portland. In the state as a whole, 28 percent of the converted land was crop land, and 42 percent forest. Close to two-thirds of the converted crop land was on prime farming soil.[3]

The Department of Land Conservation and Development contends that more than 600,000 acres of prime Willamette Valley farmland has been lost through changes in the urban growth boundary and designation of land for rural residential development.[4] Some parties identify even larger losses of farmland. According to Blair Batson of 1000 Friends of Oregon, more than 724,000 acres of prime Willamette Valley farmland has been converted to housing and industrial development since 1973. This includes 450,000 acres used for development inside UGBs, and 274,000 acres outside these boundaries where growth was not supposed to occur.[5]

These statistical studies are supported by anecdotal evidence. All around the state people report that LCDC has had only limited success in achieving its goals. Still, it has not totally failed in its efforts to save farm and forest land and prevent sprawl.

According to 1000 Friends, Oregon land law has had some achievements to its credit. Urban expansion had been taking about 30,000 acres of agricultural land each year when the 1973 law was passed. The rate of expansion had slowed to about 10,000 acres per year in the early 1990s.[6]

Mitch Rohse, Communications Manager, Oregon Department of Land Conservation and Development, pointed out that from 1987 to 1995 cities throughout Oregon expanded their urban growth boundaries 112 times, adding an additional 11,791 acres. That totals six acres per year per city, he observed, suggesting to him that UGBs continue to be a useful planning tool.[7]

So Oregon land law slowed down sprawl a bit and saved a little farm land. But it has achieved less than its sponsors expected. No one will dispute the contention that in Jackson County, Oregon, land law failed to achieve the preservation goals of those who pushed it through the legislature.

Why can the advocates of compact cities claim so little success?

EARLY DEALS AND LATER BOUNDARY FLEXIBILITY

After 1973, local governments had to delineate Urban Growth Boundaries. Many landowners at the edge of cities hoped to sell their land to developers for future development. Landowners and developers were poised to oppose a tight urban growth boundary. Environmentalists had to come to terms with them. So the parties made deals. Landowners and developers, on the one hand, and environmentalists, on the other, settled for a lot of resource land within the Urban Growth Boundary in exchange for constraints on future expansion of the city. According to Gerrit Knaap and Arthur C. Nelson, the Salem UGB was a new planning tool in 1976, and included a 25 percent surplus of land. In 1979, Portland Metro adopted a UGB

73

that LCDC acknowledged even though it thought that the UGB was too large; LCDC believed that it contained an excess of vacant land.[8] Klamath Falls also started out with a large area within its UGB.

Moreover, even after the deals were consummated, and even after an initial Urban Growth Boundary enclosed much resource land, the boundaries were not fixed and immutable. The law allowed for movement outward of a growth boundary. That is, under the law, if the advocates of city expansion demonstrated need, the Urban Growth Boundary had to be moved. Cities could expand at the expense of farm and forest land.

Before it amended its Urban Growth Boundary in 1990, Medford had 1,310 acres of vacant residential acreage within its Urban Growth Boundary. In a major amendment to its UGB, it almost doubled its vacant land for residential use, adding 1,190 acres to the total.[9] (Medford is a city with about 15,000 acres of land.)

The people who supported Senate Bill 100 and the goals of LCDC hoped for tight initial urban growth boundaries with only slow expansions of urban lands. They expected an increased population to be housed in compact cities, and they thought state officials could resist local pressures for expansion. They were disappointed.

HUNGER FOR SPACE

Oregon land law had limited success because it could not deal with intense pressures for low-density development at the edge of cities. Look at the dynamics of growth in the state.

(1) Population continues to increase in Oregon, both as a consequence of in-state births and migration

from out-of-state. The state cannot control the birth rate and it cannot fence its borders.

(2) Many people in Oregon want to live at the edge of a city.

(3) The foregoing pressures are reflected in market values of land. People are willing to pay for housing on the outskirts. Property holders are inclined to sell urban-fringe lands at the high prices that reflect demand.

(4) Developers see large profits in building on the edge of town. They employ attorneys and land-use consultants and induce local governments to annex land and zone for development either within the existing Urban Growth Boundary or within an expanded Urban Growth Boundary.

(5) Local governments respond to the pressures of residents, landowners, and developers. They want taxes and fees to get the revenues they need to supply their citizens with desired services.

(6) By its own rules, LCDC has had to accept urbanization, within existing or expanded UGBs, when the parties who want to increase the supply of buildable land demonstrate need.

So the Urban Growth Boundary is not a tight and fixed wall. Goal Fourteen, Urbanization, states that the UGB shall be based on a demonstrated need to accommodate long-range urban population growth and the need for housing, employment opportunities, and livability. The UGB has been wide and flexible; it moves outward as populations grow and as developers use their ample resources to demonstrate the need for more space on the edge of town. *Given need as a criteria for expansion of an Urban Growth Boundary, future sprawl is built into the law.*

FAILURE OF THE DREAM

How did environmentalists and legislators get it so wrong? How is it that so little farm and forest land was preserved?

Look first at the goals of the environmentalists, then compare them with the objectives of citizens in their private lives.

For the dedicated environmentalists, nature is sacred, superior to man. The goal is to preserve virtually the entire state outside the cities as empty greenspace, an area with only a few families—farmers, foresters, and park rangers, with occasional visitors from the city. Environmentalists do not object to a picturesque set of farm buildings, but they do not want to see the countryside despoiled with modern homes, garages, horsebarns, basketball hoops, doghouses, automobiles, and arterial highways. Ordinary people disturb and spoil nature.

In their private lives, however, individuals, when they can afford it, choose low-density housing on the periphery of cities. Individuals and families want to live on a piece of nature that they own, and they are willing to pay for it. Newlyweds may start in a small home on a small lot, but as soon as they build up equity and get promoted to higher paying positions, they are ready to pay for private open space. They want to sprawl out. And they like suburbia, with its handy arterial streets and convenient parking at shopping malls. They like the cars that give them choice in where they work, shop, and play.

The electorate is considerably less green than the environmentalists. It tends to oppose growth only because it dislikes the accompanying traffic congestion and city crime. After it votes in representatives that support Oregon land law, it goes out as individuals into the market for homes and chooses to live on the edge of cities.

76

Environmentalists underestimated the power of individuals in the marketplace. Potential suburban homeowners had money to spend on edge-of-city lands. Developers had capital to spend on development. The land owners and larger developers had the funds to pay attorneys and land use consultants and fight for annexation and expansion of Urban Growth Boundaries. Farmers near the end of their lives, whose children had moved to town, were eager to sell out to developers. "Scratch a farmer," say the environmentalists, "and you find a subdivider." Why not? When they were young, they thought they and their progeny would farm forever. They supported restrictive state land law. But later in life, they found themselves unhappy at the restrictions. And they were prepared to hire attorneys and land-use consultants to get out from under the restrictions. Local governments responded to local concerns.

The environmentalists overestimated the power of state and local government. Not only was the state government unable to erect a wall around the State of Oregon to keep out immigrants, and unable to impose birth control on its citizens, it was unable to contain its cities. The State was not able to contain the market forces for growth.

Environmentalists had pushed for an apparently costless containment of cities. Pass a law! Save the countryside! On its surface, this looked good to many city and country people. City people could preserve their bucolic dreams. Farmers could hope to prevent urban encroachment on their way of life. The environmentalists got the legislation they wanted because few in the state recognized the costs of preservation. In the end, almost everyone lost. Only a small amount of farm and forest lands was preserved. Some individuals got the land-use they preferred, but only after expensive struggles with government offices or expensive litigation. Others, those without money for such battles, did not get the small farm or non-farm home that they sought. Environmentalists won in the legislature, but they mostly lost in implementation of the law.

WHAT NEXT?

What happens when preservationists experienced failure, when, despite the law, low-density development occurs? They call for still more strict state controls — tighter state oversight procedures, more state enforcement orders, stricter local controls. Tighten up the urban growth boundary.

In Oregon, the cities of Ashland and Corvallis have adopted policies for a zero expansion of their Urban Growth Boundaries.[10] Mike Burton, executive officer of the Portland area Metro has not yet come out for an absolutely fixed UGB, but he writes strongly against its expansion, contending that Metro can offer its citizens a better future by not adding, every few years, 26,000 acres to the area within the urban growth boundary.[11] According to Robert Liberty, his organization, 1000 Friends of Oregon, has taken a position for a zero expansion of urban growth boundaries on exclusive farm use zones.[12]

Some devotees of the compact city even talk about shrinking the area within the Urban Growth Boundary.

. . .

What would a really compact city look like?

CHAPTER **8**

THE COMPACT CITY:
A BAD DREAM

For the environmentalist, people, buildings, and automobiles in the countryside are spillovers. They spoil the view. He or she insists that we must keep people and their artifacts in the cities.

To prevent sprawl, the authorities must make the urban growth boundary (UGB) a solid wall. Under no circumstances should urban development be allowed outside the boundary. All home construction must be within the UGB. Infill and vertical development must take the place of horizontal spread. City people are to live in tight clusters, or on top of one another in high-rise apartments. Growth in population and structures must be vertical. Suburbs are out. Private open space is verboten. If residents want to see trees and grass, they must go to a park.

In order to achieve really compact cities in Oregon, the planning authorities would have to get rid of the needs criteria that allows an expansion of the UGB. Instead of an Urban Reserve that identifies land designated for future urban development, planners would fix a permanent UGB, so that all the land outside the boundary was reserved for farms, forests and open space. Portland Metro still designates urban reserves but it also has cautiously begun to establish rural reserves.[1]

EFFICIENCY AND LIVABILITY

The compact city, its defenders argue, is efficient. The cost of infrastructure is low; the city does not have to lay water and sewer lines out to a distant periphery and the city does not have to build long arterial streets. With high population densities, the cost per passenger mile on public mass transit is low.

But look carefully at this view of efficiency! To protect farm and forest land, the preservationist is prepared to insist that people live close together. The compact city is efficient only to a person who accepts the goals and methods of the preservationists. It is efficient only to a fellow who is comfortable with the picture of a densely packed mass of urban dwellers surrounded by a relatively empty countryside. The compact city is not efficient for people who adhere to an objective of free choice, not efficient for those who want to allow people the choice of a low-density lifestyle.

The compact city is said to be livable. But livable here means living very near your neighbors, driving little, and walking a lot. A person who had to walk home with four gallons of paint might doubt the livability of the compact city. (He had to walk because the authorities "tamed" the automobile, made travel so difficult that residents could not easily drive to a shopping center.)

The compact city is advocated by environmentalists who are into control. Like the Communists in Russia and Eastern Europe, the forest and farm preservationists intend to fix the size of their cities. But up to a third of the urban populations in the Communist East European cities lived in town illegally, lived there precariously because at any time a government official could force them to leave. Rather like the poor in Southern California who, because of building constraints that lead to high-cost housing, live illegally and precariously in converted garages.

Within rigid, fixed urban growth boundaries, the price of land will be high, and will increase as population rises. Housing will be expensive. Low-income people will be out of luck.

HIGH-PRICED HOUSING

Low- and moderate-priced housing must be built where land is cheap. In the city of historical sprawl, that was at the periphery of the city. Indeed, urban planning evolved in schemes to eliminate slums through the creation of garden cities in the countryside.

If housing is to be affordable, the city must zone a great deal of land for modest homes, flat land on which the costs of construction are low. Flat land, of course, often will be farmland. But in a world of farm surpluses, the argument for protection of farmland is weak. Beginning with Malthus 200 years ago, all doomsday forecasts of unmanageable population growth and global starvation have been wrong.

When a large amount of flat land is zoned for homes, developers find that landowners compete to sell their land. The resulting low cost of land enables developers and builders to construct houses that people can afford to buy. People in modest circumstances are able to live in detached houses with fair-sized yards.

Just the opposite happens when advocates of the compact city push for "infill." They propose to limit the availability of outlying land so that new houses will be built on odd lots and small parcels scattered around town. But when a local government restricts the supply of buildable land, holders of existing parcels expect the price of their lots to rise. They hold their land off the market and speculate on a rise in its price. Fixed urban growth boundaries promote land speculation that increases the price of housing. We see it happening throughout the western United States. Workers who serve an elite that live in expensive homes cannot afford to live nearby. They have to commute for long distances, sometimes for more than 100 miles, to get from affordable housing to service jobs.

Students of public policy often assert that government should not give speculators a sure thing. A local government that consistently restricts the availability of buildable land within its borders is telling land owners that they cannot lose if they hold their land off the market.

In addition to restricting the supply of available land, Oregon land law contributes to high-cost housing through its impact on the cost of construction.

Construction costs are high on infill land, the cost of bringing in equipment for just three or four houses, the cost of workers scattered out over multiple sites, the cost of supervision. *The economies of scale in construction are lost in infill construction.*

Finally, in Oregon the elaborate procedures required to get land into the Urban Growth Boundary add to the cost of housing — procedures that include land-use studies and public hearings, public and private employee time, and the hours billed by attorneys and land-use consultants.

We can identify three ways of holding down the price of housing: One, build small houses on small lots. This, of course, gives people less value for their money. They get small yards and small houses. When the community makes available little flat land for affordable housing and that in small lots, it is telling poor people that they must get along with less space, indoors and outdoors. That is largely what the well-housed affluent in western cities have been doing in recent decades, and, surprisingly, feeling virtuous as they do it. Even so, tiny houses on tiny lots turn out not to be affordable. A second option is to subsidize housing for the poor. This band-aid solution has not done much to deal with the problem. Taxpayers are not generous with subsidy money and we find many people still poorly housed. A third alternative would be to zone a large amount of flat land for residential housing. Increase the supply of buildable land, put competition into the market for land, and lower its price. Because advocates of the compact city oppose this alternative, we must conclude that they are not serious about the housing needs of people with low incomes.

SOCIALIZED OPEN SPACE

Let's face it! Environmentalists are into control. They are determined to control how and where people live and work. "Walk, don't drive. Limit your consumption and production. Shop in nearby stores or downtown, not in a mall. Do not dwell in homogeneous suburbs. If you farm, farm full-time."

The compact city is one in which the authorities make decisions. They decide to pack people together.

What it comes down to is this: Advocates of the compact city propose to socialize open space — in parks and playgrounds, civic plazas, community gardens, supervised playgrounds, and the like. They propose to restrict building and living at the edge of the city and in the countryside. Residents cannot expect to look out their window and see open space. They must walk to a public park to look at the grass, or drive to the countryside.

Historical sprawl was different. A sprawl that promoted choice allowed *private* open space. The dweller on the rural-urban fringe could watch his children play on his own lawn. He did not have to dwell on a postage stamp lot and look at a high wood fence put in place to give him and his nearby neighbor a little privacy.

More than a few people will find my picture of a

rigidly compact city to be nightmarish. People required to live in tight clusters and on top of one another! Order! Controls! Lack of choice! Advocates of the compact city are inclined to play down the vertical urban environment consequent upon a tight Urban Growth Boundary. They do not care to be identified with Le Corbusier who proposed to house city dwellers in 700-foot towers. But, if legislators and administrators adhere to the agenda of environmentalists who are determined to house people in compact cities, life in high-rise apartments is the likely outcome for many residents.

Preservationists, moreover, do not want to compensate those who lose when open space is socialized. I deal with this "takings" issue in Chapter 14.

· · ·

We can identify two possible compromises between the advocates of the compact city and those who want to want a low-density lifestyle at the edge of town. In the next two chapters, we look at greenbelts with satellite communities and we consider an orderly sprawl.

CHAPTER **9**

GREENBELTS
WITH SATELLITE
COMMUNITIES

Consider a city surrounded by a neat band of green. Within the band, scattered houses for those who want to live in the countryside. Further out, satellite communities to absorb a rising population. Not, as in historical sprawl, greenspace that is only a random scattering of empty parcels and occasional parks. Rather, a planned use of land, a particular shape, a tidy pattern but with a good deal of free choice.

Greenbelts represent a geometric land configuration for an affluent middle class.

Not much affordable housing, however, as we will see.

PRIVATE OPEN SPACE

Open space in a greenbelt includes private as well as public lands. It comprises large lots with detached houses at the edge of the city, large yards in which children play, and, just outside the city, five- or ten-acre farms along with private woodlots. Many people, perhaps most people, like to see open space around their houses. When they settle for little private space, it is because they cannot afford more.

85

To be sure, families that live on the edge of town frequently do not pay fully for the streets and highways that they use and they may pay less than cost for the water that is delivered to their outlying locations. Sewers may be subsidized.

Advocates of the compact city use the cost of infrastructure as an argument against homes on the outskirts of the city. And those who want a vibrant downtown take a similar position. They argue that there is no reason that downtown residents should subsidize the people who chose to live on the outskirts, that there is no reason to subsidize scattered dwellings and rural roads. They insist that local governments should impose system development charges on developers to cover the capital costs of outlying infrastructure — trunk water lines, oversized sewer pipes, and arterial streets. They insist also that the authorities should charge outlying households properly for daily water consumption and sewer usage.

There are, of course, difficult problems in cost accounting when cities set charges for infrastructure, but they already deal with these in calculating present-day development fees.

Defenders of sprawl, of low-density housing, could strengthen their position were they to accept proposals to charge for the infrastructure used by distant households.

One cautionary note: Current residents ought to hesitate a bit when they insist that newcomers pay for the infrastructure that service new homes. They might consider the fact that they themselves were and are the beneficiaries of much infrastructure that they did not pay for. When they were born, most residents of the United States inherited water and sewer pipes, roads, schools, playgrounds, and much else, assets that were paid for by the people who came before them. When they move to a new city (Americans are a mobile people), they find a huge amount of infrastructure in place that they did not finance. Beneficiaries of assets left by past generations might decide that they would like to emulate their forerunners and pass on to future citizens a generous quantity of the resources that support life, including roads, water lines, and sewers at the edge of town.

. . .

A greenbelt with satellite communities would offer many households the private open space that they value. But what about communal open space, open space accessible to everyone?

PUBLIC OPEN SPACE

Men and women want local, state, and national parks. Some want public golf courses. Large constituencies exist for public forests, coastal frontage, wetlands, and wildlife habitat. Numerous citizens believe that, in addition, the government should preserve a great deal of open farmland in the countryside — cultivated fields, pastures, and range land — with only a few farm buildings scattered about. Dedicated environmentalists want to drive through an almost empty countryside.

Critics of Oregon land law argue that its supporters aim not only for greenbelts around cities, but aim to have the entire countryside a rural parkland.

Governments buy land for parks. Private land trusts purchase land for preservation as open space. (The land trust holds the land itself, in trust for the public, or it donates the land to the government.)

When the community considers land purchases for open space, it must decide how much and where it wants to have its parks and nature preserves. Some say, "the more the better." But users of greenspace experience diminishing marginal utility. As parkland is added to an existing inventory, the utility of incremental units of open space declines. Scarce land devoted to private yards, commerce, or transportation may provide greater benefits. Moreover, advocates of land preservation need to think about location and access. A national park far from large population centers is of little value to inner city residents who cannot afford to drive there. A forest or wetland that is accessible only to all-terrain vehicles is of little value to the drivers of ordinary automobiles.

One consequence, frequently overlooked, of buying land for public use, whether purchased by government agency or land trust, is that the land is removed from the tax roles. And lost tax revenues adversely affect other governmental programs such as education or public safety.

FARMLAND AS PUBLIC OPEN SPACE

The usual argument for the protection of farmland is that such protection is needed in order to assure future supplies of food and fiber. Yet, as we saw in Chapter 4, we live in a world of farm surpluses, a world in which, beginning with Malthus 200 years ago, all doomsday forecasts of unmanageable population and global starvation have been wrong.

I suspect that the real goal, seldom admitted, of many people who advocate the preservation of farmland is the preservation of scenic rural landscapes. They want to drive through the countryside and see crops in the fields and animals in the pastures. They want to see only a few buildings. They want to make farmland (rural scenery) *public* open space.

When governmental units take physical possession of land for open space, using their powers of eminent domain, they compensate the private owner. That is not the case, as we shall see, when governments protect open space by restricting private use. When a government forbids the development of a wetland area or the construction of a destination resort, it does not compensate the owner for lost value. When a government prevents farmland from being subdivided or prevents an owner from building a house on his farmland, it does not compensate him for the loss in value. We will consider this issue of property rights and taking later in Chapter 14.

A MIDDLE LANDSCAPE

When we consider the good life at the edge of a city, we are looking at an old idea in the history of city planning — greenbelts and satellite garden communities. It goes back to Ebenezer Howard, Patrick Geddes, Louis Mumford, Rexford Tugwell, Frank Lloyd Wright, and many others. Visionaries dreamed of a garden city.

Good regional planning can preserve greenspace and yet accommodate people who want to enjoy a combination of rural and urban living on the outskirts of the city. An alternative to compact cities sharply divided from open country would be cities surrounded by greenbelts, with satellite communities outside the belts. This middle landscape, combining rural and urban values, would include both public and private greenspace. In a greenbelt, one would see public parks, walking paths, wetlands and the like. One would also find large lots privately owned and, out beyond the large lots and scattered houses, small acreage for the part-time farmer. We are, of course, talking about low density housing, elbow room for the individual — empty lots on which kids can play sandlot baseball, detached houses, big gardens and big yards, yards that are play areas for children. (Mothers like to look out the window and check on their children at play. They cannot do this when the children are away at a communal playground.) Privacy is protected by distance. Residents do not hear spousal quarrels through a common wall.

Preservationists are opposed to large lots and small farms even on the outskirts of a city, "lots too large to mow, but too small to farm." They choose not to recognize that many people prefer a large lawn and a riding mower. And when they talk about lots too small to farm, they are talking about acreage too small to farm as a full-time commercial operation.

Environmentalists in Oregon, as we saw in Chapter 4, have an aversion to part-time farmers. They think of them as affluent professionals who operate "hobby" farms. They do not seem to realize that many part-time farmers are working people with jobs in towns and cities.

I write here about greenbelts, but the principles that I elucidate apply to other bounded land configurations, greenways along a river or lake frontage.

What would it take to put greenbelts around our cities?

A PROGRAM FOR GREENBELTS

(1) *Voter Mandates:* Local governments would have to have strong mandates from their voters. Only with such mandates would these governments have the will to resist increased densities in the greenbelts.

(2) *Two Lines:* Governments, acting for their communities, would have to draw *two* lines, Urban Growth Boundaries and Outer Edge Greenbelt Boundaries. When I first became aware of the need for two boundaries, I wondered what other writers on the subject of greenbelts might have said on this subject. I found out that most people who write about greenbelts are decidedly vague on just what they would look like and what would have to be done to bring them into being. After much search,

I did find a geographer, Robert E. Dickenson, who stated the matter clearly. He asserted that a planning authority has to draw up "an exact plan of the land reserved for its Green Belt. This means drawing with precision an inner boundary (around the city) and an outer boundary (in the countryside), between which will be the controlled Green Belt."[1]

(3) *Other Shapes:* The greenspace would not have to be a traditional greenbelt. It need not even be a belt. Any firmly bounded shape would serve the purpose — an oval configuration or a greenway along a river. Metro (in the Portland area) has begun to designate and bound "rural reserves" that serve as buffers between urban centers.[2]

(4) *Permanency:* Boundaries would be permanent. The greenbelt would have to be legally fenced-off, in perpetuity. Readers, at this point, will respond that "boundaries must be flexible. The world changes and land uses must change with it." The idea of fixed boundaries, however, ought not seem to be strange. Governments fix boundaries all the time, around parks, for example.

(5) *Zoning:* Communities would have to decide what they want between these two lines, what they want in their greenbelts, and then they would have to zone for it. Do they want large lots (say, one-half or one-acre lots)? Do they want small-acreage farms (of, say, five to ten acres)? Larger farms? More than likely they will want parkland, perhaps forest land, wetlands, and so forth. Communities will have to decide on the composition of their greenbelts and establish appropriate zones.

(6) *Satellite Communities with Corridors:* Governments would zone for satellite communities outside the greenbelt and establish corridors through the greenbelts for infra-structure, corridors for arterial roads ("parkways"), water lines, sewer lines, and so forth.

(7) *Development:* Governments would have to allow construction on adequate land outside the greenbelt to house a growing population and provide for the general development of suburban life. Development must be allowed outside the greenbelt to relieve pressure for development within the greenbelt and meet the preferences of people who do not want to live in a compact city. Outside development may take the form of satellite communities or even new cities.

(8) *Compensation:* To meet a widely held test of fairness, the community would have to compensate private landowners within the greenbelt for the loss of development rights. Local governments or nonprofit agencies would purchase properties outright for parks and the like and they would buy development rights from farmers. (Portland Metro does not compensate for land designated as "Rural Reserve.")

(9) *Infrastructure:* Communities would decide how to finance infrastructure within and beyond the greenbelt, employing some combination of user fees and system development charges. Fees and charges might be high for the residents in the sparsely populated greenbelt. These residents might be expected to pay well for living in the attractive surroundings within the greenbelt. Fees and charges could be lower for the more densely settled communities outside the greenbelt. The economies of scale in infrastructure supplied to these relatively dense populations might offset the costs of moving traffic, water, and waste over long distances. Some communities might even subsidize life outside the greenbelt in order to relieve population pressures on the central city and on the surrounding greenbelts.

The critical components of a greenbelt are three: a permanently bounded greenspace (an inner and outer boundary), satellite communities (to absorb population growth) and corridors (to connect the satellites to the city).

Environmentalists have been reluctant to accept satellite communities. Not willing to settle for less than a statewide, farm-forest parkland, not willing to see separate hamlets or towns, they insist on compact cities and they label unconnected communities "leapfrog" development. Decisions of households to live apart from the main city are unacceptable.

Those who value fields and forests, however, might recognize that satellite communities outside greenbelts are the best hope for preserving greenspace and absorbing an increase in population. The conversion of some rural land into satellites and corridors, might be a compromise that environmentalists and advocates of growth could both accept as a strategy for the preservation of greenspace.

CHOICE IN LIFESTYLE

Within carefully designed greenbelts and properly zoned land, developers build for the market. Families choose where and how they live.

Levies for infrastructure help to keep the city compact, not by fiat, but through use of the market. Markets give people choice. Development fees put a price on infrastructure and the prices of lots and acreage reflect these fees. The potential homeowner, constrained only by his budget, is free to choose location and lifestyle, free to choose a downtown condo, a large lot for a big yard and garden, or acreage for a small farm.

The middle way, a middle landscape between town and country.

The most striking evidence in Jackson County of failure in Oregon land law is two decades of housing built on valley farmland. A bounded greenbelt, with satellite communities and corridors, would have saved farmland in the valleys and put dwellings on the hillsides.

AFFORDABLE HOUSING, THE STILL UNRESOLVED PROBLEM

Not much low-priced housing will be found in a city with a greenbelt.

The fixed boundaries of the greenbelt will cause prices of land and housing in the city itself to rise. The cost of infrastructure (transport, water, and waste disposal) will cause the price of land to and housing in outlying satellite communities to be high. If the satellite communities are put in the hills to save farm land, housing will be still more expensive. Low-priced housing requires flat land.

All over the West, planned constraints on the supply of buildable land are raising land and housing prices. Workers have to drive long distances (often more than 100 miles) to serve city people in these exclusive communities. In Jackson Hole, Wyoming, the billionaires are driving out the millionaires, and workers have to go all the way to Dubois and Pinedale to find affordable housings.

One answer is housing subsidies, but the middle-class electorate is not likely to vote for really large subsidies for worker housing.

· · ·

Greenbelts look like a good compromise between the environmentalists and the advocate of growth. But we must recognize that they are a solution that appeals mostly to a prosperous middle-class. In the next chapter, I look at a model that might provide low-cost housing.

CHAPTER **10**

AN ORDERLY SPRAWL, A GREEN MOSAIC

When we look, with detachment, at the edge of urban communities we find that large numbers of people want to live on the periphery of a city. But old-timers on the outskirts are upset when newcomers move in and disturb their solitude. Could the quiet life at the edge of the city be made more secure? Before we address this question, however, we need to contemplate the attractions of life at the edge of town.

LIFE ON THE OUTSKIRTS

Consider the discount stores on the periphery of town. Plenty of parking, and low prices. These outlets appeal to those on tight budgets. The discount store, to be sure, does not provide variety. It mostly stocks high-volume products, and provides minimal service.

Those who do want variety and service go to the shopping mall. I am not sure why the liberal-left looks down on the mall. Perhaps because of its "wasteland of parking space." Elitists drive automobiles, but they want ordinary people to ride the bus.

Take a closer look at the mall. It is, in important respects, a walkable city. It is a *pedestrian* mall, but it is, with its abundant parking, at the same time, a structure friendly to the automobile driver. The mall provides much of what

95

people move to the city to find, proximity and variety. Specialty stores, with an emphasis on service. Movies, arcades, and other recreation. Restaurants. And even in some cases a private social service agency or civic presence (like a state employment office). Malls sponsor art exhibits, choir performances, and festivals. They are places with a variety of stores and activities, they are localities for teenagers to hang out (the modern-day equivalent of the corner drugstore), and localities where retirees take mall walks.

Environmentalists tend to decry materialism, consumerism. They value wildlife and wetlands, and scenic views. But people, environmentalists included, get much of their satisfaction from the simple comforts of daily life—automatic washers and driers, crisp vegetables from the refrigerator, handy meals from the microwave, attractive clothes from the store, easy parking at the mall. Suburbanites want commerce to be close to their edge-of-city residential life and semi-rural pursuits. Accessible commerce enhances the low-density housing that many people prefer.

Sprawl is a loaded word. A sprawling city is disorderly. Sometimes I have thought that we should drop the expression. Use a neutral term. Call the sprawling city a city with a low-density periphery. The word "sprawl", however, may indeed point to the essence of one kind of urban living. The city that sprawls supports individualism, individual free choice, a considerable measure of anarchy. At its edge, such a city has a variety of *private* open space—empty lots, large lots, and small acreage for the part-time farmer.

THE EFFICIENT AUTOMOBILE

Advocates of the compact city speak of America's "love affair with the automobile." It is, they suggest, an adolescent, immature attachment. When Americans mature, they will walk or ride their bicycles.

Most people who walk and ride bikes, however, do so for health and recreation. When they work, they drive their cars, their efficient cars. Whether it be paid employment or volunteer activities, they accomplish more when they drive. They drive to work, they drive to the office, they drive when they do routine shopping, go to the bank, and run errands.

Consider the idealist who volunteers to help the poor or protect the environment. She wants to do good. But she quickly realizes that she can do a lot more good per unit of time by driving her car than by walking, bicycling, or riding the bus. An automobile is efficient. It takes the driver door to door, and it saves time. A person does not have to walk to the bus line, wait for the bus, wait while the bus stops for other passengers, and then walk to his or her destination. Time is money, says the businessman; time is doing good, notes the volunteer. The best mass transit cannot duplicate the efficiency of the automobile.

People have different goals and they want to do different things. Sprawl gives people choice in where they live, downtown or at the edge of a city. The private automobile gives people choice as to whom they will visit and where they will shop. The automobile as a working vehicle is efficient in its promotion of individual choice.

Those who put down the automobile ought to consider why it is that car pools have had so little success. Homes are scattered around town. People work at different places and have different work hours. Schools open and close at different times. Schedules differ. Errands are a problem. (People in car pools cannot stop for errands along the way to or from work. If they do so, they inconvenience the people with whom they share the ride.) On some days, a participant in a car pool has to stay in town for an evening meeting, or he wants to take in a play. The private automobile gives individuals and families choice that they cannot get from the communal car pool.

Mass transit is even less suited than the car pool to serve individual differences. It is of necessity set up to serve the routine.

Anyone who looks at life on the edge of cities and the role of the automobile in modern life must take into account not only the efficiency of the automobile but the reality that, for many people, driving is fun. Advocates of individual choice can argue that government agencies should look not only at the preferences of environmentalists who favor pedestrian walks, bicycle paths, and mass transit but also should consider the preferences of people who get pleasure from driving.

DOWNTOWN IS NOT AUTOMOBILE FRIENDLY

The city is valued for proximity and diversity. People live in town or come to town because stores, offices, repair shops, banks, and so forth. All are close together. Customers can choose from a variety of goods and services. Workers find a choice of jobs; manufacturers find a work force with a variety of skills. People come to the city for recreation; teenagers (and some not so young) are attracted by the bright lights.

But people hate driving downtown with its congested streets and inadequate parking. The central city is not friendly to the individual who arrives in a car. So people move out to the edge of the city. And, unless subsidized, the inner city decays and is left to sleaze and crime.

Accessible commerce and low-density housing appeal. When a dweller returns from the mall to his home on the rural-urban fringe, he can look out of his window and see a considerable expanse of greenspace. He need not dwell on a postage stamp lot and look out at a privacy fence.

RURAL ZONING

We saw that the anarchy of historical sprawl causes serious difficulties for the individual who moves out to the edge of town. He settles in, happy in his isolation, only to find out that, sooner or later, others, seeking solitude, move in next to him. Lacking foresight, or money, he failed to buy a big enough piece of land to keep others at a distance. He did not, or could not, buy land for protection.

People who fear that newcomers will crowd them and clog their streets have legitimate concerns. Not in my rural retreat, not in my small town, not in my back yard. "Nimby" (individual or collective), is understandable.

We can identify a solution to the dilemma of people who move to the outskirts to find peace, then want to keep others from following them into their chosen areas. The solution is to *plan* for sprawl, plan for an orderly sprawl, a green mosaic.

A community can designate territory for low-density life styles. Zone in the city for large lots. Zone outside the city for one-, five-, ten-, twenty-, or thirty-acre parcels. Come to an agreement on terrain for rural residential uses, for small commercial farms, and for hobby farms.

Rural zones are set up to minimize spillovers. People who move into zones with suitable minimum parcel sizes need worry little about obtrusive or noisy neighbors, structures that cut off their view, congested roads, falling water tables, and so forth. Zoning can be supplemented by regulations that limit spillovers — noise ordinances, weed ordinances, restrictions on run-off into streams.

Plans may include buffers between zones when uses are incompatible.

Even as people want protection from the unpleasant or harmful activities of adjacent landowners, they want their own preferences to be met. How can this happen?

In their zoning decisions, both the authorities and the developers can respond to market forces. The authorities do their best to forecast the market for different land uses and zone adequate land for each of the alternatives. Developers, in a similar manner, forecast demand for particular land uses, then lay out land and construct buildings accordingly. Consumers buy land and housing that meet their preferences.

Within community zoning constraints and individual budget constraints, people choose freely where and how they live.

If residents at the edge of town are to be secure, if they are to be certain that new structures will be kept at a distance, zones must be stable. Zoning changes must be rare. When, however, zoning changes are inescapable and expectations are disappointed, fairness calls for compensation. And in a changing world, some zone changes cannot be avoided.

What about public greenspace? Governments can buy land for parks, playgrounds, or nature preserves. Or they can buy development rights if they want some farms for city kids to look at. Riverside County in Southern California has a park made up of orange groves. Public open space is scattered about, perhaps in a sort of checkerboard — not even with the regularity of a mosaic, just a random scattering. Orderly sprawl does not bound the city with a greenbelt that limits the availability of buildable land at the edge of town.

LOW-COST HOUSING

In the historical sprawling city, builders constructed a lot of modest homes on good-sized lots. Because new land was readily annexed, land for housing was cheap. Cities installed utilities and laid out roads that might even be dirt or gravel with drainage ditches at the sides. One never heard the words "affordable housing." Low-priced housing just happened, supplied by the market out on the edge of town. *The authorities did not restrict the supply of buildable land.* Indeed, it may well be that only in a sprawling city will low-income wage earners find housing that they can afford. Certainly they will not find it in the compact city, discussed in Chapter 8, and probably not in a city bounded by a greenbelt, the configuration we dealt with in Chapter 9.

ORDERLY SPRAWL: BETWEEN ANARCHY AND AUTHORITY

Imagine a world in which the electorate and the authorities have escaped the Malthusian myopia. People do not believe that government must save farm and forest land. Land use is determined partly by zoning but mostly by the market.

The critical features of orderly sprawl are stable zoning, on the one hand, and the free purchase and sale of land, on the other.

Rural land would be preserved. It would be preserved, however, not by directive, not by fiat, but in response to market forecasts, forecasts of demand for the products of small- and large-scale agriculture and forecasts of demand for rural residences.

At the same time, developers could supply low-priced housing, starter homes and rental units. They would bid flat land, necessary for affordable housing, away from farmers when the housing benefits (relative to costs) exceed the benefits (relative to costs) of additional food and fiber.

Households are free to choose. Live in town on a small lot or live on the periphery on a small farm. Enterprises

101

are free to respond to market-revealed preferences. The community exercises a measure of control. Government deals with the problems created by spillovers — through rural zoning, regulation, and perhaps buffer zones.

The individualist gives up the anarchy of the frontier, where the newcomer could move in on the old-timer and disrupt his solitude. Zones that set minimum parcel size protect the person who wants to live apart. This is the countryside for the heirs of the individualists who pioneered the American frontier, who broke the prairie, then often moved to the edge of town to live out their old age. But the frontier has been domesticated with limited regulation and careful zoning.

In sprawl, albeit orderly, the affluent middle class forgoes the neat geometry of a greenbelt.

The community serves equity with compensation for zone changes (changes that take away options which a purchaser in good faith thought he had acquired). The case for compensation is strong when land is down- or up-zoned. If, when he bought his land, a householder could reasonably have expected a lot of greenspace around him but then allowable densities in his area were increased, he is entitled to compensation. If, at time of purchase, a buyer could reasonably have expected to subdivide his land into small parcels, he has a claim for compensation when the community denies him this option.

Builders construct affordable housing on low-priced flat land on the outskirts, unrestricted by a tight boundary around the city.

Orderly sprawl is quite different from a greenbelt. Having forgone the neat geometry of a strip of green, it allows growth but at the same time makes possible affordable housing. The tidy-minded might prefer greenbelts but free spirits will choose a perhaps less tidy green mosaic.

C H A P T E R 11

EXCLUSIVE ENCLAVES FOR THE AFFLUENT

Many of those who support restrictions on Oregon land have a simple, albeit seldom stated, goal — preservation of an empty countryside. They want to drive down the highway and see fields and forests, with few dwellings. Unable to keep people from entering the state, they propose to confine them in towns and cities.

Critics of development testify against the expansion of Urban Growth Boundaries. They fight annexations and subdivisions, and do what they can to limit building permits. When local officials respond to citizens who want to live on the periphery, critics call in the powers of the state Land Conservation and Development Commission (LCDC).

To be sure, opponents of development do not want to look like they are selfish, look like they care only about their own surroundings. So they speak in the name of the physical environment. Preserve open space, green space, wetlands, and scenic views. Protect farm land, lest the people starve, and protect forests, lest wild life suffer. They play on fears.

Preservationists are nostalgic for the past: They speak of a small-town atmosphere, a walkable city, bicycle paths. "Livable" towns, for them, are the surroundings of their youth.

Consider Governor McCall's famous, or infamous, statement: "Come visit us again and again. This is a state of excitement. But for heaven's sake, don't come here to live."[1] We want the profits of tourism. We do not want more neighbors. Listen to the voices at public hearings: "I like Talent the way it is." (Children speak like this when they do not want to share their toys.)

Preservationists ignore critics who point out that they are speculating on a rise in their own property values. (Restrictions on the supply of buildable land increase the price of already platted land and increase the value of existing homes.) Preservationists also ignore critics who note that the high price of land in a compact city is a good way to keep out poor people and minorities.

Where do the votes come from that so firmly support Oregon's exclusionary land laws? Dedicated environmentalists themselves are not that numerous. And the ordinary citizen is not very green. But, while he is not a strong environmentalist, the average householder hates road congestion and fears urban crime. So he votes for candidates who promise to restrict growth and discourage people who might otherwise settle in the area.

Keeping people out is most of what Oregon land law is about. The most striking evidence of this is the way LCDC looks at size and efficiency in agriculture. We looked at LCDC's bias against small-scale agriculture in Chapter 4, but let us pursue this subject a little further.

Suppose LCDC could not care less about efficiency in agriculture. Suppose that its only objective was the preservation of a statewide parkland, a countryside with few residents and fewer buildings. What administrative rules might it enact? How about a minimum parcel rule of 80 acres (160 acres for rangeland)? And a house construction rule that requires a gross income not less than $80,000? Nothing in the rule that deals with the cost of farming different-sized parcels. Nothing that recognizes the elementary economics of net income as a measure of efficiency.

Is it not clear that keeping people out is the underlying motivation of the supporters of Oregon land law? Upholders of this law really are inhospitable. As they restrict the numbers of homes and keep up the price of urban land, they create exclusive enclaves for the affluent.

AN ALTERNATIVE, MORE GENEROUS, VISION

Environmentalists are into "vision," green fields, lofty forests, beautiful vistas.

But consider an alternative dream: A community that shares, that welcomes newcomers. A community that encourages growth so that it provides jobs and resources, family-wage jobs and resources with which to increase choice for its residents (along with resources with which to help the disadvantaged).

"We do not want to be like Orange County," assert the opponents of growth. But the early settlers in Orange County did share their land and attractive climate with others. They did not, as soon as they arrived, shut the door to followers.

A vision for moderates. Reject the moveable Urban Growth Boundary, the failed LCDC model that only raises the price of land and housing! Reject what is now coming to the fore, the authoritarian, rigidly-fixed, growth boundary! Instead, choose either a planned greenbelt with satellite communities or an orderly sprawl with affordable housing — a middle landscape with large lots and small acreage, rural living on the outskirts of the city, perhaps something close to the traditional egalitarian frontier.

. . .

Whether crowded into cities or spread out over the countryside, residents have to address the issue of road and highway congestion. In the next chapter, I look at the use of land for the transport of goods and the movement of people.

CHAPTER **12**

THE USE OF LAND FOR TRANSPORT

The major goal of an agency that plans transportation is to expedite the movement of people and goods, either through improvements in the flow of goods on existing arteries or through the construction of new facilities. Today, however, some agencies seem to have another agenda. They want to check the expansion of the transportation system; they want to limit infrastructure in order to protect greenspace and promote compact cities.

IMPROVED TRAFFIC FLOWS

Transport planners reduce traffic congestion through coordination of traffic signals, correction of alignment deficiencies, restriping lanes, construction of turn lanes, designating one-way streets, and so forth. They smooth out traffic flows and reduce delays in order to reduce the frustration of drivers. Do they also plan for higher speeds and higher speed limits, so that people can get from one place to another more quickly? Perhaps in some cases. But today few highway planners show interest in increasing the velocity of automobiles. They seem to join the foes of automobile travel and act to "tame" the automobile.

TRANSPORT PLANS TO CHECK SPRAWL

Travel is to be multi-modal. And the goal of the planner is to discourage solitary travel, which is considered to be anti-social. The community will tell people how to get about. Do not travel alone! Do not drive your car! Ride the train or bus! Share your ride! Join a carpool! Ride a bicycle, or walk!

In 1970, the authorities in Eugene, Oregon wanted people to walk. They closed off twelve downtown blocks and created a pedestrian mall. But residents preferred suburban malls and major stores left the center of the city. So by 1996, Eugene had decided to spend $1.8 million to reopen downtown to automobiles![1] The lesson? Transport planners err when they do not think clearly about the role of the automobile.

What, then, may we ask, are the prospects for all those bikeways and sidewalks that planners want to build? In modern times, people who ride bicycles and walk do so mostly for recreation. They seldom consider walking or bicycling to work, for they know that leg-power is slow. If they bicycle to the office, they arrive tired and sweaty. How many people, then, will actually use the bikeways and sidewalks that are being built? The authorities cannot order people to walk or bike to work, and not many individuals will leave their cars at home. So the cost per bike- or pedestrian-mile of bike paths, wide highway shoulders, and sidewalks will be high. Proposals to put resources into paths and walkways represents a nostalgia for a lost, simpler past.

The advocates of compact cities want to design transport systems that discourage travel. They want a grid pattern of streets, neo-traditional designs with many intersections to slow down traffic. Arterial highways are to be limited, streets narrowed. Environmentalists call it "taming the automobile" or "traffic calming." In reality, it is taming people, drivers and passengers, restricting their choices. Cars do not have volition. At the extreme, environmentalists advocate parallel parking in lieu of angle parking. They like the idea of an individual bringing autos behind him to a halt while he works his way into the curb.

Intersections in grid systems do slow down automobiles, but they add to the number of accidents — unless, of course, the authorities install stop signs at all the intersections and slow down traffic even more.

CONGESTION PRICING

Transport planners have been slow to consider the use of price in the allocation of road space. They mostly look for a combination of engineering and regulations to deal with congestion. But, when use of road space is virtually free, no community can build its way out of traffic jams. Because of growth in the automobile population and the popularity of automobile travel, there is a huge pent-up demand for streets and highways — the unsatisfied demand of people sitting at home, choosing not to fight the traffic. As fast as new roads are constructed, drivers get into their cars and fill up this new capacity.

A far more promising approach is to price road travel. The city of Singapore is pioneering in what is sometimes called "electronic road pricing." Other labels for this approach are "congestion pricing, "time and place road pricing," or simply "road pricing."

In the following paragraphs, I describe a future transportation system that is, at present, barely beyond the blueprint stage.

Roadside units send out signals that identify particular streets or intersections and their current prices. Each vehicle is fitted with an "in-vehicle unit" that picks up these signals, records the position of the car at each moment in time, and records the current price of the piece of road on which it is moving. For cash, a driver buys a "smart card" and inserts it in his unit. The card contains encrypted credits from which travel charges are deducted as he moves about the city or through the countryside. When the credits on a card are about to be used up, the driver purchases a new card. Alternatively, a driver obtains a personal billing travel card, a travel credit card, and pays for his use of streets and highways at the end of the month.

The price of each piece of road varies with location and time of day—high prices for popular expressways and for use during rush hours, low prices for less-used routes and for non-peak hours. Prices are, insofar as possible, market-clearing, prices that equate quantity supplied (road capacity) with quantity demanded (vehicles on the road). Ideally, congestion disappears.

Road pricing generates funds for the construction and maintenance of roads, and frees general tax revenues for other uses. Forecasts of revenues and outlays are used in decisions on road construction. Prices (forecasted prices) paid by drivers provide a measure of consumer travel preferences, while (forecasted) costs of equipment depreciation, materials (portland cement, gravel, and sand) and labor measure the value of alternative uses of construction resources. (To be sure, forecasts of prices and costs are imperfect measures, but they are better than no attempts to measure likely benefits and forgone alternatives.) Anticipated revenues support the sale of revenue bonds; actual revenues can be used to finance maintenance in accordance with usage. Heavily-used routes get more maintenance funds.

Congestion pricing would provide both short- and long-run benefits. In the short run, drivers respond by changing their driving patterns. Businessmen and workers purchase roadway time during the rush hours. Retirees travel at mid-morning, mid-afternoon, or during the evening. Men and women who value their time purchase travel on busy routes; those with time on their hands buy low-cost travel on less-used streets. In the long run, enterprises and households relocate. They move closer to one another, so as to minimize travel charges.

Road pricing would promote efficiency. It would reduce or, ideally, eliminate congestion. People would not waste time in traffic jams. Pricing travel and the movement of goods would curtail these activities and decrease the number and width of roads that have to be built. Road pricing encourages public mass transit — light rail and bus travel. Mass transit need not be subsidized. Congestion pricing also shifts freight traffic back to the more efficient railroad. (The lack of road pricing subsidizes over-the-road trucking.) When market prices are used in making investment decisions, the system as a whole is more efficient.

Why are we only now beginning to consider attaching prices to the use of roads? Because, when people think about markets, they think only about capitalism. Road-pricing is market socialism, about which the general public knows little. But just as efficiency is served by market-clearing prices in the private sector, so is efficiency promoted by the use of price in the governmental sector.

Needless to say, efforts to move toward congestion pricing encounters opposition. For one thing, it runs into vested interests. People oppose paying for something they now get free. However, once it is understood, congestion pricing may be the basis for compromise between con-servatives and liberals.

Conservatives are likely to approve a market system that promotes free choice, a system in which those who receive benefits pay for them. Conservatives also may recognize that traffic congestion is a major factor generating support for environmentalism. The ordinary voter is only a little bit green, but as he sits in a traffic jam, he becomes an environmentalist. So conservatives might want to push a scheme that reduces the appeal of the environmentalist agenda.

Liberals will defend congestion pricing when they come to recognize that it would reduce travel, reduce exhaust pollution, decrease the need for land devoted to roads, and promote compact cities. The Transportation Issues Coordinator of the Sierra Club in Oregon has cautiously suggested that environmentalists look at electronic road pricing.[2]

1000 Friends of Oregon advocates congestion pricing (which it calls peak-hour pricing) as a way to reduce vehicle miles traveled and increase the use of public transit. It does not recognize that road prices should vary in space nor does it recognize that congestion pricing would give travelers free choice in mode of travel.[3] Freedom of choice in the use of land has not been a 1000 Friends goal.

TRANSITIONAL DIFFICULTIES

Application of electronic road pricing will encounter one major problem. Our streets and highways are laid in concrete, mostly fixed in place for the indefinite future. A rapid "big bang" movement to market-clearing road prices would cause horrendous disruptions. Prices on the most congested highways, intersections, and on-ramps would go sky high. Particularly would road prices skyrocket when lower-priced routes were not available or far out of the way. Middle-class travelers would go into shock. Low-income workers could not afford to drive to work. Residents on alternative routes, encountering a lot of traffic on roads that were not built for arterial use, would be unhappy.

This does not tell us that congestion pricing is an unsatisfactory long-run goal. It does suggest that the transition from virtually free roads to roads that require payment for use will be long one. It may take a century or two (after the public understands its desirability) before congestion pricing could be widely used.

In the meantime, the authorities can develop transport plans that move in the right direction. New roads can be constructed with the intention of an immediate or later charge for their use.. The authorities can start with low initial prices and gradually raise them toward levels that clear the market. Planners might consider the gradual introduction of electronic pricing on particularly congested highways or at bottleneck intersections.

As a transition to congestion pricing, simple mileage charges can be used. The authorities might read odometers once a year and charge drivers accordingly. Note that present-day toll roads charge by the mile.

More toll roads can be constructed. Tolls can vary with time of day. A highway in suburban Los Angeles, a new ten-mile strip of four commuter lanes, will collect tolls electronically as cars drive by. In this experiment in congestion pricing, motorists at peak hours are to pay $2.50, higher than the minimum charge at other times of $0.25.[4]

A tax on mileage is a less sophisticated measure for dealing with congestion than road prices that equate supply and demand at different points in space and time. Such a charge only reduces automobile travel generally. It does not differentiate different parts of the road system; it does not so well address the problems of congestion.

Critics are concerned by the impact of road pricing on low-income people. They worry about members of the working poor that have to drive to work. Low-income drivers, however, can be helped with "highway stamps," like food stamps. To be sure, travel subsidies such as these should be time-limited. The long-run objective is to get workers to move closer to their work (and get employers to move closer to their work force).

Although the problems of a transition to electronic road pricing are serious, the benefits are so great that sophisticated transportation agencies will set this as their ultimate goal. They will recognize that eventually the community must price scarce road space.

In the meantime, motor fuel taxes serve as a crude way of charging for street and highway use. Those who understand the role of price in transit, its role in equating the quantity supplied with the quantity demanded, will lobby for higher gasoline prices as a substitute for road pricing.

LIMITS ON ROAD CONSTRUCTION TO CHECK GROWTH

In Goal 9, Economic Development, the Land Conservation and Development Commission (LCDC) states that "plans should designate the type and level of public facilities and services appropriate to support the degree of economic development being proposed." In Goal 12, Transportation, LCDC asserts that "the planning and development of transportation facilities in rural areas should discourage urban growth . . ." According to LCDC, the goal of transport planners should be to limit, not facilitate, movement. Planners, it believes, must keep people out of the countryside.

In the latter part of 1995, Oregon Governor John Kitzhaber added the Oregon Department of Transportation to the forces that are to check growth. He directed ODOT to use its powers to preserve farm and forest land.

TRANSPORTATION IN SOUTHERN OREGON

The Rogue Valley Council of Governments, in 1995, began to draft a Regional Transportation Plan. Transport planners, having identified goals, and aware of spillovers, proposed to minimize air, water, and noise pollution, and to minimize the impact of transportation systems on existing neighborhoods. They also wanted to maximize the safety of the system.

One plan goal was to "improve the efficiency of the existing transportation infrastructure"; another was to "maximize the efficiency of the transportation system." Under the heading of "transportation systems management," the planners proposed to reduce congestion through coordination of traffic signals, correction of alignment deficiencies, and so forth. Those who drafted the plan sought to reduce travel time. Reduction of travel time might be achieved in either of two ways: (1) through the reduction of congestion delays or (2) through the achievement of higher speeds. There is no evidence, however, that the planners sought to increase the velocity of automobile traffic. The plan was to tame the automobile driver.

When the people who drafted the Rogue Valley Transportation Plan turned to "transportation demand management," they assumed that transportation resources are fixed in supply. Their explicit goal was to "reduce travel demand" through (1) reduction in the total quantity of travel, (2) reduction in individual travel, and (3) reduction in motorized travel. They proposed to reduce total travel by promotion of telecommuting and the four-day work week. Individual travel was to be reduced by an increase in transit use and by carpooling. And motorized travel was to be cut by an increase in facilities for pedestrians and bicyclists — more sidewalks and bikeways.

115

Perhaps the most striking feature of the draft transportation plan is this emphasis on the *management* of demand. No one seems to have considered that consumer demand might call for expanding highway availability, that planners might want to find out what consumers of travel want and then respond to the their preferences. The draft plan fails to consider evidence that Americans like the mobility that their cars provide. In sum, research on consumer preferences for transportation is not a part of transport planning.

It seems clear that the people who drafted the Rogue Valley transportation plan have responded to the ideology of the compact city. A low-density life style is bad, automobiles are bad. Residents in the valley must preserve farm and forest land, live close together, drive less and walk more.

If the most striking feature of the draft transportation plan is its emphasis on demand management rather than research on consumer demand, the most striking omission is its failure even to mention congestion pricing. The plan suggests parking charges and fees as incentives, but it does not recognize that charges for automobile movement would be the most effective way of dealing with congestion.

Finally, a word about parking charges. Just as Americans think that their streets and highways should be free, so they think that parking should be free. The Regional Transportation Plan does consider that parking charges have value, but it sees them only as disincentives that shift people out of single-occupant autos. Parking fees, however, do more than this; they offer choice to drivers. Market-clearing prices on space used for parking serve the same purpose as market-clearing prices on space used for movement. They reduce congestion and free up space. People do not have to drive around the block looking for a place to park. Parking space is not rationed.

Drivers can park in a space as long as they want, provided that they are willing to pay a price that reflects its scarcity. Like road charges, parking charges give people free choice and promote efficiency in the use of scarce land resources.

. . .

A time may come when the electorate recognizes that price has a role in the public sector as well as in the private economy.

CHAPTER **13**

DEVELOPMENT, AN AFTERTHOUGHT

The Land Conservation and Development Commission, of course, is supposed to concern itself with economic development. It does so, but in a strikingly limited way. It considers growth, but only within compact cities. LCDC does not consider the forgone growth possibilities that occur when it prevents the transfer of land from rural to urban pursuits.

GROWTH AS AN OBJECTIVE

Often people are affronted at the allegation that they oppose economic development. They do accept growth, provided that it is managed, or provided it occurs some-where else. Controlled growth or growth at a distance.

Some people, however, are opposed to all growth. They are complacent, satisfied with the world in which they find themselves. Pleasantly situated in a small town, with a good shopping center a few miles away (not too close, not too far), they like the idea of an environment that does not change. "I like Ashland the way it is."

A considerable opposition to growth comes from in-dividuals who have a narrow view of what constitutes growth. When they think of growth, they think only of increases in marketable goods, consumption goods and the factories that turn them out. Growth to them represents consumerism. Materialism!

Growth that includes an increase in capital (both capital goods and human capital), however, may change the world for the better in many ways. Growth may improve housing for the poor, provide better school buildings for children, train teachers and social workers, improve nursing homes, reconstruct decrepit bridges, and so forth. Growth may provide resources for changes of particular concern to environmentalists, resources for cleaning up pollution sites, resources to line irrigation ditches, reclaim wetlands, fence riparian areas, even remove dams and restore free-flowing streams. Non-marketable resources are included in measures of growth through the use of cost-benefit analysis.

Growth increases value, wealth. That which is prized may be marketable products, consumer goods and capital goods as measured by the prices that individuals and firms place on these goods. Or, the things valued may be resources that seldom or never enter the market place — the skills of a musician, the birds in an old-growth forest, the beauty of distant vista.

The only people who can rationally oppose growth are the totally complacent, those for whom all that exists is good and for whom all change is bad.

GROWTH IN CITIES

In its Goal 9, Economic Development, The Land Conservation and Development Commission (LCDC) deals mostly with expansion in urban areas. It looks at cities and concludes that "a principal determinant in planning for major industrial and commercial developments should be the comparative advantage of the region within which the development would be located." Plans should promote "those economic activities which represent the most efficient use of resources" in a geographic area.

LCDC also recognizes that, in cities, comprehensive plans should based on current market forces. Plans should consider labor market factors such as educational technical training programs. Plans should take into account the availability of key public facilities and provide for an adequate supply of sites for industrial and commercial uses.

Perhaps the greatest inadequacy of Oregon land law is the restraints that it places on changes from rural to urban activities.

GROWTH, BUT NOT ON RURAL LAND

Neither in Goal 9 nor in its Guidelines does LCDC recognize that comparative advantage should be considered in deciding between city activities and farming. It also does not allow market forces to operate in decisions that impact the transition from rural to urban pursuits.

The reasons for these omissions, of course, are a preoccupation with future supplies of food and fiber along with desires to keep residents and buildings out of the countryside. Unfounded fears about distant future events cause Oregon planners to ignore the adverse consequences of farmland protection on prospects for growth. LCDC fails to recognize that comparative advantage and the forces of the market call for conversion of farm land to urban uses, and that restrictions on such conversions checks economic development.

Perhaps it is the nature of planners to distrust the market. While many, if not most economists (along with developers, realtors and businessmen generally) embrace the concept of the "highest and best use" for land, planners are inclined to believe that they know best what is the best way to use resources.

Consider an economy without government protection of farmland. As populations grow, as technology makes it possible for fewer people to grow the nation's food and fiber, people move to town. Urban pursuits contribute more to the good life than do rural activities. The present values of the products of the city are greater than the present values of the output of farm and forest. Much land is now more productive when switched from agriculture to manufacturing, commerce, finance, or services. Land is best employed where it has the greatest comparative advantage.

When Oregon land law inhibits a change from agriculture to urban uses, people lose out. Resources are misallocated and people are deprived of necessities and amenities that would improve their lives.

Far from markets, experiencing the competition of domestic and foreign suppliers, the pear and apple orchards of the Rogue River Valley are losing money. Field and row crops likewise are uneconomic. Yet Oregon land law stands in the way of converting farmland in the Valley to urban pursuits. Protection of a failing agriculture is responsible for high land prices in Rogue Valley cities and is a burden on commerce and industry.

THE CARRYING CAPACITY MYTH

Much cited by environmentalists, the concept of "carrying capacity" is used to limit growth. In the Guidelines to Goal 9: Economic Development, LCDC asserts that "plans directed toward diversification and improvement of the economy of the planning area should consider, as a major determinant, the carrying capacity of the air, land, and water resources of the planning area." The same admonition is to be found in the Guidelines for Goal 6: Air, Water and Land Resource Quality. The concept of carrying capacity suggests that the capacity of any given area to support a given population is fixed, fixed by the availability of water and other natural resources. But the supply of water and other resources in any location is a function of price. When the price is high enough to cover the cost of shipment, water, minerals, and other materials are delivered to places where they are needed. Water is short in some localities because it is inappropriately priced — too low to attract supplies (and too low to induce people to economize on its use).

The world is full of water. Seventy percent of the globe is covered by oceans. Huge bodies of fresh water and vast numbers of running streams cover the land. In recent times, more and more recipients get part of their water delivered from desalination plants. And, as I have said earlier, men have been transporting water throughout the ages. We know of the Roman aqueducts. Arabs used to carry water across the desert in animal skins; now they haul it in trucks. In my town of Ashland, many believe that virtually the only available water is in the nearby Ashland Creek. Water from the Rogue River, however, could be purchased from the Medford Water Commission and brought to the city by pipeline.

Water can be treated as a commodity, bought and sold. To be sure, reliance on the purchase of distant water carries some risks. Physical interruptions may occur, earthquakes or civil disorders. Economic, political, or legal factors may interrupt deliveries. Another valley may bid for the water and raise its price, perhaps so high as to make it prohibitive. Another jurisdiction might win a political battle for water deliveries. A court decision might give water rights to a competitive user.

These risks lead some observers to advocate watershed self-sufficiency. Communities ought not rely on water deliveries from over the hill.

Critics of the market have always pointed out that there are risks in reliance on market forces. They have advocated self-sufficient farms, self-sufficient towns, self-sufficient regions, or self-sufficient nations. But trade has immensely raised the standard of living of the people who have relied on markets. Ultimately, a citizenry has to decide between the security of self-sufficiency and the growth and higher standards of living associated with trade in market economies.

One other point. As development occurs, as people move to the cities and engage in urban pursuits and as land is transferred from agricultural to urban uses, water can be released from farm irrigation and becomes available for city production and consumption. The supply curve for water need not be a fixed vertical line. When water is not impossibly far away, its supply curve can slope upward and to the right, as do most supply curves. A higher price may increase the quantity of water supplied. In Chapter 4, I discuss in detail water transfers from agricultural to urban uses.

When the possibilities of transportation are considered, the capacity of any area to support a given population is seldom fixed. The notion of a fixed carrying capacity is, for most regions, dubious economics.

THE COSTS OF FORGONE DEVELOPMENT

Those who support restrictive land laws do not look seriously at the issue of growth. One hears the statement, "Hopefully the goals of farmland protection and economic growth do not conflict." They do conflict. Farmland protection prevents the transfer of land to growth-generating urban pursuits. And much of what people want for the future depends on economic development.

North Americans see themselves as rich, yet look at

their immense, present-day, wants. Men and women want more and better consumption goods, vehicles that give them mobility, labor-saving appliances, housing that shelters them from the elements. The critics of consumerism are the relatively affluent who are already well supplied with material goods. People with modest incomes, to say nothing of the poor, have huge unsatisfied wants.

The homeless desire shelter. Yet high prices on land, caused by restrictions on the conversion of farm land to housing uses, contribute to homelessness.

And then there are the deprived who live in the inner cities. Vast resources are wanted for more and better social workers, more and better teachers, more and better policemen. Enormous resources are needed to refurbish and replace inhospitable high-rise public tenements, fix up run-down school buildings, and clean up dilapidated parks.

Everyone worries about the costs of caring for the aged, a growing part of the population. The costs of medical care continue to rise. People look at the prices charged by nursing homes, and fear the future.

Mental health programs are in shambles for lack of resources. State institutions have been emptied out, but community programs have not been developed in their place.

Infrastructure throughout the country is in disrepair — streets and highways, bridges, water pipes, sewers. Many buildings need to be retrofitted so they might withstand earthquakes.

The costs of cleaning up Superfund sites boggles the mind — toxic waste, chemical solvents, heavy metals.

A word about "growth management." If managed growth means that urban development is allowed only in appropriate zones, zones that prevent spillovers from adversely affecting neighbors, few will object. If, however, managed growth places limits on development in urban settings by restricting the availability of accessible water or by restricting the availability of land for industry, commerce, and housing, then the cost of growth management will be high.

The state of Oregon, the nation, nations everywhere, have an almost desperate need for growth. Only in a developing economy will the resources be available to meet the immense needs of a growing and aging population. Many of these needs can be met by the private sector. But some can be met only by government. People, however, will not vote for taxes if they find themselves in a stagnant economy.

LCDC needs to look more thoughtfully at the last two words in its title, "Economic Development." It needs to recognize that growth mostly results from decisions made by individuals, actors in autonomous enterprises. These decisions, in modern times, are made, to a large extent, in urban centers. Expansion mostly takes place in cities. Because farmland protection prevents the transfer of land, capital and labor from agriculture to urban pursuits, it obstructs economic development. The consequences of growth forgone are extremely serious.

CHAPTER 14

TAKINGS AND WINDFALL GAINS

When government agencies take physical possession of land, they must, under the Fifth Amendment to the U.S. Constitution, compensate the private owner. If a city takes possession of land for a park or a school district takes land for a school, the city or the district has to pay the private owner fair market value for the land.

In recent years, a new issue has come to the fore. Government agencies frequently leave landowners in physical occupancy but drastically restrict the ways they can use their land. To preserve wetlands, an agency, on behalf of the community, forbids construction of a lodge. To preserve an empty countryside, an agency forbids subdivision or forbids construction of rural dwellings. In such cases, under present law, the government need not compensate the private owner for his or her loss of value. This is the "takings" issue.

The controversy over property rights and "takings" has aroused passions on both sides. Let me put the reader on guard. Neither conservatives nor liberals will be entirely satisfied with my analysis of this subject. The matter is terribly complex. Can we measure values lost as a consequence of regulations? Can we identify and measure windfall gains (economic rents)? What is just? At the end of the chapter, I speak for caution.

WHAT IS PROPERTY?

The word "property" has two meanings. In ordinary usage, it refers to a tangible object—a house, a barn, or a tractor. An irate homeowner asserts that "this kid damaged my property when he hit his ball through my window." He perceives property as a physical object, a window. In law, however, property is a set of rights (courts call it a "bundle of rights"): the right to income from a bond, the right to sell a house, the right to post land against hunters.

The two meanings of property often are confused. A critic of factory layoffs argues, "I believe in human rights, not property rights." But property rights *are* human rights. A factory building has no rights. Its owner, a human being, has rights. He may have the right to close down the plant. A worker, likewise human, has rights to his own body. Courts protect his rights to join his or her fellow workers in a walkout.

Failure to recognize the two meanings of the word "property" confuses the issue of compensation for lost value. The courts hold that a physical taking must be compensated. If a governmental unit takes physical possession of a piece of land, so that the private owner loses all rights of use, courts insist that he be compensated with money equal to fair market value. If, however, the individual can still walk on the land, if he can still occupy the site, but can do little else with it because of government regulations, the courts (so far) have held that he is not entitled to compensation. Such an action is not a "taking" protected by the Fifth Amendment. A government agency may take, without compensation, virtually all of the set of rights that make up the bundle, if it leaves the owner in physical possession.

When the courts focus on property as a physical object, they forget that, legally, property is a bundle of rights, of which physical possession is only one. That is, when they look only at the right of occupancy, they ignore all the other rights of an owner.

Indeed, what has happened is that the courts have allowed governments to socialize a large part of what was private property in land, and socialize it without compensation. A legislature or administrative agency, on behalf of society, can take most of the rights of the landowner away and leave him only minor rights of use.

Now, for many readers, critical use of the word "socialism" will be perceived as bad form, illiberal, "red-baiting". But use of the word socialism, precisely defined, may help us to understand the significance of private property in land. Socialism (def.): Government ownership and administration of the means of production (land and capital). The community as a whole owns and controls the means of production.

Under socialism in Western Europe and the Soviet Union, people in government decided on the use of resources. Under Oregon land law, government officials decide whether land can be devoted to urban pursuits. In both cases, government officials, not private parties, decide. In both cases, the mechanisms for decision can accurately be described as socialism.

Traditional socialists recognize virtually no individual rights. They dislike private property, and, insofar as they think about rights at all, they think only about the rights of society. Present-day environmentalists are not complete socialists. They do accept the rights of physical possession, the rights of an owner, say, to walk upon his or her land. And they accept the contention that if a government takes away all the rights of physical possession, it should compensate the owner. But environmentalists are prepared to leave to land owners little more than incidental rights of casual use. They do not believe that individuals should have rights to cut trees, terrace hillsides, drain wetlands, divide land, build houses, and the like. Loss of such options, they argue, need not be compensated. Environmentalists would compensate only for a complete taking and they oppose compensation for a partial taking, no matter how great.

Democratic socialists in Europe compensated owners when they socialized enterprises. Totalitarian socialists in the Soviet Union did not compensate individuals for the loss of private property. One day Oregonians (who are unwilling to compensate for an almost-complete socialization of land) might become uncomfortable with the company they keep.

A century of experiments with socialism, in many countries, has checked economic development. That is why almost everywhere, societies have been engaged in privatization. Constraints in Oregon on the private use of land almost certainly act to reduce the rate of growth in the State.

Both conservatives and liberals confuse the takings issue.

Ideological conservatives suggest that the rights of private property are absolute. An owner, they argue, should be free to do whatever he or she wants with his or her possessions. The law, however, has always limited the rights of ownership. An owner of an axe may not strike another person with this tool. An landowner may not divert runoff water on his land to his neighbor's farm.

Liberal environmentalists confuse the takings issue by their failure to distinguish between two kinds of government actions — governmental actions to *check spillovers* and government actions to *preserve* resources. That is, they fail to distinguish between spillover issues and preservation issues. When the community, acting through government, tells a property owner that he may not spew smoke over the countryside or spill toxic waste into a stream, the community is insisting that he behave as a good neighbor. Few would argue that he should be compensated for loss of a "right" to be inconsiderate of the people around him.

Environmentalists use these spillover examples, however, to argue against compensation for community insistence that a person preserve a resource. They oppose compensation for government directives that require a private owner to preserve a farm site, a wetland, a forest, or an orchard, even though directives impose large losses on individuals.

Thoughtful people will ignore the ideologues on the two sides of the issue, the extreme conservatives who argue that property rights are absolute and the extreme liberals who would give the community unlimited powers over individual preferences.

Moderate conservatives probably will agree that the community can act to protect unique land sites (lake frontage, wildlife habitat, and the like) but argue that either the community should purchase the land, should pay market value for it, or that it should pay the owner for lost development rights. As critics of uncompensated restrictions, they will ask why one individual, the property holder, should suffer losses on behalf of the entire community.

Liberals will respond that purchasers of land often know that a governmental body intends to acquire it for public use, or that they know (or should have known) that the community would insist on preservation of a beautiful scenic view.

Judges who rule on compensation disputes might choose to look at the time of purchase and the expectations that the parties had when they consummated the deal. Suppose that the logging of a piece of forest land is challenged. How long had the property been owned?

When it was purchased, did the law and the customs of the day assume that property owners could cut down trees at will? How long had adjacent residents owned their land and what were their expectations at the time of purchase? Could they have reasonably expected that the forest and the viewscape would remain intact in the foreseeable future?

Suppose that according to law and prevailing customs when the properties were purchased, forestry companies were expected to preserve views. Then constraints on their timber cutting might be justified. Suppose, on the other hand, property rights at the time of purchase included the right to alter the view. The timber company might properly expect compensation if now required to forego large profits to protect a viewscape. (An alternative might be that the community purchase a wide right-of-way along a road in order to have a screen of trees along a greenway.)

We should not be surprised, however, to find preservationists opposed to compensation (and opposed to purchases of greenspace). They realize that voters would elect fewer environmentally-friendly legislators if these voters knew that they would, through the taxes they pay, have to compensate losers from new acts of preservation.

Environmentalists give two reasons for their opposition to compensation. One, the landowner is a steward of the land and should preserve its natural attributes. Two, increases in land values are windfall gains and do not represent landowner contributions.

NATURE AND STEWARDSHIP

Environmentalists contend that human beings cannot own nature. But what do they mean when they say this? They cannot mean that individuals, on their own initiative, may make no changes whatever on their land. They would not defend the proposition that individuals, as opposed to society, can have no rights of decision with respect to trees, shrubs, grasses, or anything that is green. Environmentalists almost certainly do not intend to socialize everything that might be labeled "nature."

Perhaps what environmentalists mean when they assert that people cannot own nature is to be found in what they write about stewardship. They may simply want to add the concept of stewardship to that of property. The landowner, they contend, is a steward. But to whom is a steward responsible? And what are his responsibilities?

Most people would expect a steward to feel an obligation toward his family. They would expect him to take care of family assets. But most men and women also would want a steward to give some consideration to the neighbors. They would not want his actions to spill over into adverse consequences for the adjacent households. Communities pass environmental laws to deal with those who think only of themselves, laws that require individuals to avoid spillovers. Individuals and enterprises are not allowed to pollute streams that flow through their lands or let weeds grow up and go to seed.

So much for stewardship and spillovers. What about stewardship and preservation? A steward is expected to husband the family's resources on behalf of his children and heirs. But should he also be expected to preserve natural resources in his possession for the benefit of future society? Can he be expected to forgo early uses, beneficial to himself and his family, on behalf of the community? Can the community require this steward of a family's patrimony to forgo its development on behalf of the community, and not compensate him for the lost value associated with restrictions on its use?

WINDFALL GAINS .

A relatively new, and yet not so new, argument against compensation is the contention that increases in land values are unearned increments, windfall gains. Land is not produced by human beings, environmentalists point out, and increased values of private land often reflect population increases and economic development on surrounding lands. So the community may take these values without compensation. We are back to an interesting piece of history, back to the story of two Georges, Henry George and Lloyd George.

Henry George (1839–97), an economist, recognized that land was different from capital. Location, pure site value, is not created by man; it is a free gift of nature. A choice waterfront site is not a product of human labor, investment, or risk-taking. It is a creation of the Gods. The return to land is a rent, a surplus. So Henry George argued for a tax on land rent, a single tax. (He proposed to abolish taxes on capital and labor.)

A detached analyst must recognize that men and women do not produce site value, do not produce, say, all the value of the only waterfront land in a city. The problem, however, is that the value of a scarce site is mixed with the value of human improvements. How to separate the two? The treatment of land value is a complex matter and requires much thought.

A homesteader stakes out a claim to 160 acres of land. Thirty years later he sells it for $20,000. Some of this value is a consequence of the fact the people moved in around him and a town developed a few miles away. But part of the value represents his work. He cleared the land, drained a swamp, fenced it, built a house and a barn. How does the analyst separate the results of community development and the results of his labor?

Moreover, land is seldom held by the original owner, the person who settled on it in pioneering days. That person sold it long ago, and over the years it has passed through many hands. The present landholder purchased it in good faith, in most cases with money he earned through the provision of goods or services. Take an owner who bought land for $30,000 and sells it for $80,000. The initial investment of $30,000 may well have represented a return to labor or saving or risk-taking. What about the gain of $50,000? Is it an unearned income, a windfall profit? To be sure, he may have done nothing with the land during the interim. But while he held the land idle, the owner may have kept an inappropriate structure from being built on it, perhaps prevented construction of a store building on a site that would be better used for a civic structure. The proprietor may have been a developer who waited for the land to ripen and meanwhile kept it out of inappropriate uses. He or she may also have drained the land, terraced it, put in sewer pipe, and in other ways improved the surface. Now how much of the $50,000 gain in value reflects what economists call economic rent, a surplus, and how much is a return to entrepreneurial risk-taking and capital formation?

Lloyd George (1863–1945), the liberal English statesman, did not propose to capture all of the land rent, all of the presumed surplus that resides in this free gift of nature. He proposed to tax only the "unearned increment," the increase in value of unique sites attributable to population growth. He wanted to capture the value that was not a consequence of actions by the owners of property. But he too failed to consider the problem of separating earned from unearned returns.

While he holds it, an owner's investment in land and improvements is at risk. (The owner may be a small holder or he may be a large developer.) The value of any

134

piece of land may fall. History is replete with examples of land booms that collapsed. It may well be that most of an increase in value can be attributed to the developer's forecasts of future growth, his activities in preparation for that growth, and the risks he took.

Still, some of the return to landowners may be attributable to an unanticipated growth in population and seen as an unearned income that might be taxed away or taken by regulation, without damage to incentives. The person who acquired the property just happened to be in the right place at the right time; he or she lucked out, and got a windfall profit. But capitalism, indeed life everywhere, is full of windfall gains. Look at some other gains attributable to chance.

Children with a good genetic inheritance, born of loving parents in an affluent suburb, educated in good schools, these children receive high incomes in later life. Their subsequent high earnings can be described as windfall gains. Economists call them "rents of ability." Think of the high billing fees of an able attorney, the consulting fees of a gifted automotive engineer, the salary of a basketball star, the income of a top official in an environmental organization.

At times the modest investor and the ordinary worker receive gains of luck. A person invests in a small coffee shop in an old part of town. Then tastes change. The area is gentrified, and his coffeehouse becomes popular with a large clientele. He cleans up. Or a carpenter locates in a small town. Investors develop a ski resort nearby and the town grows into a major destination resort. Now his skills are in great demand and his earnings high. A not insignificant part of the goods and services that people enjoy are simply the results of good fortune.

Even when the community can be almost sure that increases in the value of a parcel of land are a consequence of nearby developments, it might prefer that the individual profit by the sale of his land. For years he was allowed to hold the land and pay taxes on it in the expectation that he could sell it and use the proceeds to pay for care in his old age. As a matter of public policy, communities often recognize such claims with a "grandfather's clause." The law even recognizes "squatter's rights," when a person has occupied land for a long period with no legal challenge. Western jurisprudence, frequently protects people from disappointment attributable to a changes in public policy. Indeed, concerns about disappointed buyer expectations were one of the factors leading to the 1993 passage of Oregon House Bill 3661. The bill allowed individuals to construct a dwelling on land that they had purchased in good faith, in the expectation that they would be allowed to build.

An unthinking taking of what is believed to be un-earned income may have a bad influence on the social fabric. The individual who experiences a taking sees it as a breach of faith. He invested in land in the expectation that he would be allowed to develop it, or at least build a house on it. Now the community says he cannot do so. He gets angry. "I was prudent and saved. I worked hard all my life. Over the years, I delivered crops of good food to the community. Now that I want to retire, sell my land, and move to town, I find the value of my land much re-duced by unexpected regulations."

MODERATION AND PRAGMATISM

A direct, comprehensive money tax on windfall gains, on unearned increment in land values, is not politically acceptable. For more than a century, the small but dedi-cated followers of Henry George have pushed for a land tax. Only rarely have they caught the attention of the public. And only in a few cases have taxes on land rent or levies on unearned increment been enacted.

Indeed, in practice, communities frequently act in such a way as to benefit particular individuals and businesses, and do not try to capture these private gains. A state locates a college in a particular town, and benefits nearby households. The government does not attempt to tax away the individual benefits.

Just as communities are slow to tax unearned gains, they are slow to compensate when government actions hurt individuals, when, for example, zoning decisions reduce the market value of urban land. Governments do not compensate for the adverse consequences of zone changes and the courts allow considerable loss of value without compensation. New York City led the way in the zoning of city land. Its comprehensive zoning resolution of 1916 was carefully designed to be part of a general police power, safeguarding "public welfare" and "public health, safety, morals and convenience." As a consequence of this skillful drafting, the City did not have to pay compensation as it did when it used its powers of compulsory purchase.[1]

To be sure, we do find some levies on unearned increments and some compensation for undeserved decrements.

While comprehensive levies on unearned increments have generally been rejected by the public, occasional levies on unearned benefits are part of the system. Governments impose special assessments on landowners whose property goes up in value when they improve a street (when they pave the street or put in curbs and gutters). More recently, system development charges have become the levy of choice as a source of funds for infrastructure. These development charges almost certainly capture a part of the Georgian unearned increment in land values. Some governments try, quite conscientiously, to identify the "area of benefit" and levy charges accordingly.

We also find instances of compensation when public policy changes and individuals are hurt. After tariff reductions in the Sixties (the "Kennedy round"), the federal government compensated enterprises and workers hurt by increased imports. After restrictions were imposed on timber harvests in the Northwest, workers and others were given governmental assistance under the federal Northwest Economic Adjustment Initiative.

With measurement problems so serious, a careful community would attempt to capture apparently unearned gains only when they were decidedly unearned. The same community would compensate only when a considerable loss of value had occurred. Indeed, moderate conservatives propose to compensate losses that result from regulation only when the loss in value exceeds a certain amount, say, ten percent.

We live in a world in which gains and losses reflect merit and demerit, good and bad luck, and much in between. Wealth and income may reflect work, savings and investment, or they reflect sheer luck, unexpected population growth, or favorable changes in public policy. Losses in wealth and income may reflect bad forecasts, or indolence, or error, or bad luck, or adverse changes in public policy.

A pragmatist recognizes that there is much to be said for simplicity, for keeping taxation and governmental expenditure simple. A tortuous effort to identify and tax all the gains that are unearned or identify and compensate all the losses that are undeserved would create an unmanageably complex system.

A moderate, pragmatic approach to the takings issue will disappoint ideologues on both sides of the issue. But untidy compromises are at the heart of democracy.

WHEN GROWTH IS AN OBJECTIVE

In a world of scarcity and privation, arguments for an emphasis on economic development carry a lot of weight.

A community concerned with growth would be careful in its decisions to tax, or take away by regulation, what it suspects are windfall gains. It does not want inadvertently to eliminate rewards for foresight, effort, and risk-taking. The almost inevitable mistakes of government can adversely affect incentives.

Any community would do well to recognize that the possibility of gains associated with pure luck may itself stimulate effort and risk-taking. Joseph A. Schumpeter in Capitalism, Socialism, and Democracy called the prizes and penalties of capitalism an "enticing admixture of chance" and he pointed out that most businessmen receive only modest compensation or even lose money. Yet, with the big prizes before their eyes and overrating their chances of success, they continue to do their utmost.[2]

When a governmental agency takes property without compensation, it frequently is treating it as a free good, failing to consider the cost in forgone alternatives. Consider this example: When government takes by regulation, without compensation, seventy acres of land around a nesting place for a pair of spotted owls, it need not consider the cost in forgone lumber that might have gone into the construction of homes. When, without compensation, it forbids the subdivision of farmland near a city, it need not consider the cost in forgone urban products that suburban homeowners could have turned out.

A community concerned with growth will encourage the developer, a person, small or large, who acts as a representative of the future needs of a growing population. He, risk-taker as well as a mover and shaker, represents the young couple who hope, as their family grows, to move up to a larger and better home. He represents the absent person who in future years will move into the area, a person who otherwise would be unrepresented in land-use decisions. Indeed, the developer, as he pours concrete and lays trunk sewer lines, not seldom represents the unborn children of the future.

The power to regulate is the power to destroy incentives. The institutions of capitalism are not perfect. But private property in a free-market economy has been an extraordinary engine of growth in large parts of the world. Much of what we want to do — alleviate poverty, care for the elderly, refurbish infrastructure, clean up toxic waste — depends on continued growth. A mindless taking of property rights threatens to undermine a mechanism that has done much to lift the burden of poverty from the shoulders of mankind.

CHAPTER **15**

THE HEAVY HAND
OF THE STATE

If it is to limit spillovers, a community must constrain individual land-use decisions. But at what level of government will zones be delineated, regulations enacted, and site-specific decisions be made? Will such matters be left to the counties and cities, or will state officials restrain private land-use decisions? When the legislature passed Senate Bill 100 in 1973, Oregon tried to have it both ways. A state agency would establish goals and set guidelines while counties and cities would draw up comprehensive plans and regulate the uses of land within their jurisdictions. In the end, however, the Land Conservation and Development Commission (LCDC), acting through its administrative arm, the Department of Land Conservation and Development (DLCD), became more powerful than many expected.

Control remains an issue today, however, as local governments struggle to maintain control over the land under their jurisdiction and state agencies fight to defend their powers.

Advocates of local control contend that local officials, those who serve the local community, are likely to do a better job of enacting land-use constraints than distant officials in the state capitol.

THE CASE FOR LOCAL CONTROL

County commissioners and city council members know their areas better than people in state agencies who are far away. They know better what resources are available in the locality. They know the soil characteristics and the topography. They know the existing road networks and the local businesses. Local officials know about spillovers in the locality and know better what their constituents want in the way of preservation and conservation as well as growth, jobs, housing, schools and parks. Population densities and industry, commerce, and jobs, all are concerns of the people who vote them into office.

Residents of Southern Oregon ask why distant collective bodies in the Willamette Valley should tell them where and how they should live.

Still, some things are matters of statewide concern.

THE CASE FOR STATE CONTROL

When it is a matter of spillovers that cross jurisdictional lines, the state must be involved. But that is the rub. What are the matters that transcend local boundaries? How define matters of statewide concern?

Some cases are clear cut. If smoke from industries in one region spills over into another, the state must curb the miscreant. But what about traffic from a shopping center that spills over and impacts residents in an adjacent region? How much traffic and what kind of traffic (autos, heavy trucks) should get the state involved?

Perhaps the best that can be managed is to define "matters of statewide concern" by example. List matters that are and that are not matters of state concern. Then qualify with the word "major" all items on the list. State authorities may involve themselves only in *major* traffic problems, *major* waste disposal, *major* watershed issues, and so forth. In addition, in order to protect local and regional autonomy, the legislature might insist that the *burden of proof* be on any state agency that proposes to intervene in what the local citizenry consider to be purely a local affair.

One of the arguments, in 1973, that persuaded legislators to enact strong land laws was the contention that only state government could contain pressures for growth. Developers, and landowners who want to sell to developers, it was argued, put immense pressures on local authorities. Developers and subdividing farmers were seen as bad guys who think only of money. Together they overpower county commissioners so that the latter allow subdivisions to spread out through the countryside.

This argument should be recognized for what it is, a cynical view of democracy, a cynical view of the electorate. It suggests that people do not know what is good for them, that they cannot cope with individuals and businessmen who come in with money and proposals for change. Colonialists for centuries have argued that indigenous people do not know what is good for them. We, the elite, they have argued, take care of the people. And Southern and Eastern Oregonians sometimes think of themselves as colonies dominated by Portland and Salem.

Historically, colonialists found local people, usually tribal minorities, who would support them and carry out their wishes. The British did so in Africa and Asia. The authorities in the Willamette Valley have found locals to assist them in Southern Oregon, the Jackson County Citizens League (an affiliate of 1000 Friends of Oregon).

The case for local control is the case for democracy, for limited government. It is a local application of the concept of federalism. Limit the powers of distant government officials who do not understand local concerns.

143

ON ADMINISTRATIVE LAW AND BUREAUCRACY

Advocates of a large role for the state in land-use matters want strong state government. They seldom, however, think seriously about administrative law and the nature of bureaucracy.

When it encounters a problem, a legislature cannot pass a simple law and then expect it to administer itself. A legislature cannot, for example, simply require cities and counties to adopt comprehensive land-use plans and then enact appropriate land-use regulations. The issues are too complex for a short and clear state law. The legislature will have to create an agency, like the Land Conservation and Development Commission, to implement the law. The agency then decides just what should be in a comprehensive plan and what sort of regulations will adequately enforce it. It supplements the initial legislation with a body of administrative law. As time passes, local governments figure out ways to get around the regulations that do not fit their circumstances. To deal with these evasions of the law, the state agency enacts still more administrative rules. Administrative law grows and the agency to enforce it grows. What started out as a simple idea, "we must deal with the environmental impact of land-use decisions," becomes a huge apparatus of administrative law, complete with hearings, paperwork, red-tape, and litigation.

Legislative and administrative bodies often use words that require value judgments when they are applied in particular situations. LCDC does this when it uses the words, "livability" and "need." Laws that reflect value preferences invite conflicting interpretations. Local and state officials arrive at different decisions when their values conflict.

In the guidelines to Goal 14: Urbanization, LCDC states that "urban growth boundaries shall be established" which consider the "*need* for housing opportunities, employment opportunities, and *livability* (my italics)." County commissioners and city council members must incorporate these guidelines into their comprehensive plans. When decisions have to be made on whether or not to expand an Urban Growth Boundary or annex land, developers and the opponents of growth debate the issues of livability and need.

Value judgments are not scientific statements. They are not objective statements that can be tested by observation of facts. When the term "need" is used, it is part of a value judgment, as in the Goal 10 statement that suitable land should be provided to meet "the housing needs of households of all income levels." LCDC attaches some value to housing, but it does not indicate how much or what kind of housing will meet household needs. So a local body, or DLCD (the administrative arm of LCDC) must convert housing needs into a precise statement of quantity, quality, and price. Someone must specify:

(1) Household categories, perhaps low-, medium- and high-income households.

(2) The numbers of households in each category (a forecast).

(3) The kinds of housing to be made available in each category, and the prices of each.

Statements of desired housing types and prices rest on non-scientific value judgments.

Consider the following: A developer asks a city to annex 40 acres of land. On the land, he proposes to build 160 houses. Forty homes will be 1,200 square feet with three bedrooms and two baths, and will sell for about $125,000. The remaining 120 houses will be 1,800 square feet, with three bedrooms, two baths, and a family room. They will sell for about $175,000.

The City Council, guided by its Planning Commission, accepts the proposal and annexes the land. It concludes that the land and the housing are "needed." It has made value judgments as to the kind of housing that is desirable in the city. In addition, believing that developers build in response to anticipated household preferences, the Council also has made a value judgment that construction should respond to the individual preferences of homebuyers. Finally, with approval of a plan for only four houses per acre, the Council has demonstrated that it values low densities at the periphery of the city.

Now, at the state level, LCDC/DLCD overrules the local authority. It contends that the developer has not demonstrated "need." LCDC believes that its preferences rather than local preferences should control, and it values compact cities.

When lawmakers enact law stated in general terms, when they enact law that includes value judgments, they give administrative bodies discretion. And when LCDC is free to overrule local bodies, it can impose its own values on local populations.

Most people find out about bureaucracy only when they have to file an application and deal with red tape and rigid officials. They think about the thicket of administrative law only when they themselves struggle to get a decision or struggle to reverse a decision made by a remote official in an inner office. (The person at the counter in a government agency has little discretion.) With little or no experience of dealing with difficult administrators and with little knowledge of administrative law and its implementation, activists in land conservation approve of government officials that they hope will keep their opponents in check.

146

The reality is that state agency officials often are over-worked, poorly paid, and badly informed. They know less about local conditions than city and county officials. They make decisions by looking at a map, when local officials can readily go out and look at the land. Administrative law is rigid and often inappropriate for a particular local-ity. In its very nature, it covers only the typical situation. One size has to fit all.

Too few people are aware of the costs that adminis-trative law imposes on an economy. Consider regulations that deal with land development: bonding mandates, den-sity constraints, required greenspace, paving requirements for streets, curbs, and sidewalks, constraints on storm-water management, requirements for sanitary sewers, engineering certification, obligatory environmental impact statements, enforcement of wetland preservation and mitigation, mandated tree preservation and planting, landscape rules, rules for hillside construction, grading permits, building permits, and so forth. The prices of homes and other buildings must cover the costs of paper-work and red-tape, along with the costs of the salaries and fees of the many attorneys, judges, and consultants who have to deal with ambiguities in the law. The meters of expensive attorneys run for hours as they sit and wait their turns to testify at lengthy hearings.

The costs of delay alone are high, the costs of deferred bureaucratic and judicial decisions. Not only do those who must wait for permission experience frustration ("justice delayed is justice denied"), but potential users forgo bene-fits while they wait for a governmental body or court to decide. Then, in addition, often they must pay higher costs for materials as a consequence of inflation.

Legislative and administrative land-use law is a large burden on economic growth in Oregon.

Finally, administrative rules, once on the books, are

hard to change. Bureaucracies defend their turf, and the parties that benefit from administrative decisions emerge as vested interests in defense of the status quo. Mistakes built into legislative or administrative law are hard to dislodge. Look at just one example: LCDC concluded that only large commercial farms were efficient. It published regulations that limited the division of land and limited building of homes on small parcels. Large farmers, thereafter, opposed change in the regulations. They did not want the competition of small farmers and they wanted to continue to purchase or rent land at low prices (land that was on the market because of prohibitions on home construction).

Advocates of state land law emphasize citizen involvement, but citizen involvement in state decisions is not a substitute for local control. To be sure, when citizens are consulted, state laws may be less oppressive. But state laws and their administrative progeny still are administered by distant officials. Citizen involvement may be likened to the committee work that administrators give potential critics of their actions: "Get them into committee work; get them into citizen involvement. That will keep them out of our hair."

THE JACKSON COUNTY CITIZENS LEAGUE

Having suggested that the Land Conservation and Development Commission has too much power, we need to look at the fact that some county commissioners exercise considerably more discretion than others. Josephine, Douglas, and Klamath counties tend to ignore LCDC, at least on smaller land-use decisions. Partly this may be because they are far from Salem. Partly it may be because DLCD, the administrative arm of LCDC, has a limited budget and limited personnel with which to police the state. Perhaps, however, it is because these counties lack strong environmental movements.

In counties like Jackson County, where environmentalists are strong, the mandates of LCDC weigh heavily. Environmentalists get themselves appointed to county and city planning commissions; at times they help to appoint environmentally-friendly local planning staff. Sympathetic local planning commissions and local planning staff may work closely with LCDC/DLCD and strongly advise elected officials to accept its decisions. When efforts to free land for development occur, environmentalists in the Jackson County Citizens League call down the powers of LCDC. Then the preferences of a local majority may be defeated by the power of the State.

. . .

For some matters, the power to decide probably should not be in either the state capital or in local governments. The capital is too far away and local governments are too parochial. Some decisions should be made by a regional planning body, which is the subject of my next chapter.

CHAPTER **16**

REGIONAL PLANNING

When local governments decide on permissible uses for land, they often fail to consider the consequences of their actions on nearby jurisdictions. State agencies might fill the gap, might coordinate or control local decisions. But frequently these agencies are out of touch; they do not know enough about local resources and local preferences. As a consequence of failures in coordination, officials and citizens in Jackson County became interested in regional planning. Skeptics, however, expressed fears that regional planning would simply create another layer of bureaucracy.

PLANNING BY CONSENSUS

Counties, cities, fire districts, water districts, and other jurisdictions often get together informally, work out their differences, and coordinate their actions. When it works, informal coordination may be the best alternative. People take into account the concerns of one another and find solutions that meet their diverse needs. Frequently, however, informal coordination fails. Disagreeable groups or individuals hold out, insist on going their own way, and disregard the adverse consequences of their decisions on others. Ideologues and zealots stand their ground.

Formal structures devoted to consensus help. In Southern Oregon, the Rogue Valley Council of Governments facilitates coordination. At its monthly meetings, representatives of member governments attempt to deal with matters that cut across jurisdictional lines. Regular meetings build understanding and trust. RVCOG professional staff provides advice and assistance. Federal and state agencies encourage cooperation by funding activities (like services to the elderly) through Councils of Government. So, hoping to share in these funds, local agencies participate in Councils.

Still, voluntary coordination has its limits. Cities are jealous of their autonomy and frequently ignore the concerns of neighboring jurisdictions.

CITIZEN-BASED PLANNING

In Jackson County, residents (worried by a lack of regional coordination) organized to engage in some sort of planning. The movement started with a group called "2050," citizens concerned about water availability, who got together to see if they could find common ground on controversial issues. Their successes encouraged people concerned with land-use issues to try a similar approach. The Rogue Valley Council of Governments helped them get started with their sessions, and the State of Oregon provided some money. Soon thirty or forty people regularly gathered to meet in a general meeting and in a variety of subgroups. They represented a wide array of interests and viewpoints and ordinarily would not have spent much time together. Their activities reveal much about efforts to plan on a regional basis.

For months, controversial matters were approached gingerly. No one wanted to spoil the good feelings that everyone had about getting together with opponents. Skeptical participants feared that the group would never get beyond touchy-feely stuff, that it would fall apart as

151

soon as serious issues were addressed. What were these issues?

Environmentalists wanted to preserve greenspace and advocated compact cities. They worried about sprawl. Preservationists did not want to see farmland used for roads that would only make it easier to build at the edge of cities. Other, however, were concerned with mobility and did want roads in the countryside. Developers wanted to build homes at the edge of cities to meet the demands of a growing population.

Advocates of growth cautiously suggested that economic development would provide the goods and services that everyone wanted as well as provide jobs. Opponents politely argued for preserving the small-town atmosphere of present-day life in the Rogue Valley. Remember, everyone is still trying to preserve harmony.

Occasionally articulated were disagreements between those who were into control and those who believed in free choice. One fellow would say, "We have to decide where we will put the new people who come to live in the Valley." And opponents would ask, "Why don't we give people choices on where they live?"

No one knew quite what to call this collection of people who regularly assembled. Someone finally labeled it "Our Group." The name stuck.

Participants could not agree on where all this talk would lead. Some expressed the view that in the end the group could and would make site-specific decisions on land use. Skeptics found it difficult to believe that such an amorphous group could decide on anything. How would "Our Group" decide? Would they vote? Who would vote? The people who showed up at the time of decision? What about existing elected bodies that currently had power? When and how would they be involved? Everyone knew that sooner or later, a decision-making structure would have to be created. But this issue was too hot to settle. A lot of people danced around it, then walked away.

And "Our Group" talked, and talked, and talked. Eventually it concluded that it would, indeed, have to have some sort of decision mechanism for itself. Within its ranks, serious advocates of regional planning knew that sooner or later a regional authority would have to be established.

The people from Medford, however, feared that they would be outnumbered and outvoted by the ten small towns in Jackson County. The small towns feared the weight of the gorilla, Medford. Those who had to deal with officials on a daily basis feared another layer of bureaucracy.

A REGIONAL PLANNING AUTHORITY

Authority. Directives. Government. Power. Who decides?

People who advocate regional planning start out with a list of land uses that they believe should be covered by a regional plan — transportation, waste disposal, industrial parks, commercial centers, shopping centers, and so forth. But such a list puts no limits on a regional body. Believers in free choice want firm limits on the authority of officials who plan. How can this to be achieved?

One proposal is that a legislature or electorate might set limits on a regional authority with a statement that *regional planning should deal only with matters of regional significance.* Regional planning should confine itself to matters that spill over from one jurisdiction to another. But when is a matter regionally significant? No one would argue that the regional body should concern itself with the location of each and every side street, or the layout of each shopping facility in its area. Perhaps the proposition could include a qualifier, "major." A regional body should deal only with *major* transportation arteries and the like. Such a qualification helps, but not much. What is major?

I see only one further possibility. Those concerned to limit the power of a regional body might insist that, in all matters of jurisdiction, the burden of proof should lie with the regional body. An act that creates a regional planning agency might state that "all powers not assigned to the Regional Planning Authority are reserved to local governments and districts" (words similar to the words in the Tenth Amendment to the U.S. Constitution that were designed to protect powers of the states). In all cases a planning agency would have to justify its contention that a particular matter is of regional significance.

Still, there is little reason to be confident that even well-chosen words can fence in a government agency once it is created. Look at how the powers of the government of the United States were expanded through the use of the commerce clause.

Those concerned about concentrations of power might hope that the courts would check a planning body that overreaches itself. But the ultimate check, the only real limit, on governmental power is an educated electorate that insists on limited government.

STRUCTURE

Regional planning by consensus is slow, and extremely limited. Much of the time, the uncoordinated decisions of entrenched local governments continue to prevail.

Effective regional planning requires an *authority*, a regional planning authority, albeit one of limited power. The state legislature or a regional electorate will have to decide how members of the authority are chosen and whom they represent. Will they be appointed? Will they be elected at large or will they be elected by the residents of designated districts? Will members of a regional planning commission represent the region generally or will they represent the districts where they live? Would they have to live in the district from which they were elected?

Whoever creates the planning authority will have to decide on voting formulas. Large cities fear that the many small jurisdictions will outvote them. Small cities fear that the big cities will dominate a planning body. The parties will have to agree on a formula for weighted voting. Fearful jurisdictions must be given the powers of a blocking vote. Suppose Medford were given 34 percent of the votes when decisions on substantive issues required a two-thirds majority. No decision could be made without its concurrence. Medford, on the other hand, would have to persuade small towns with 33 percent of the votes to vote with it before it could get what it wanted.

What about the fear that a regional authority will force citizens to deal with another layer of bureaucracy? If this is not to happen, the regional planning authority *will have to be given powers that are taken away from bodies above and below it, from state agencies like the Land Conservation and Development Commission (LCDC) and from local governments (counties, cities, service districts, and so forth)*. Each of these bodies, of course, will fight to defend its turf.

. . .

In Oregon, the big issue that divides people who contemplate regional planning is growth versus preservation.

EMPHASIS ON GROWTH AND CHOICE

Advocates of growth see markets as the principal mechanism by which men and women satisfy their preferences.

If economic development is the goal, planners will be instructed to minimize constraints on business enterprise and local jurisdictions, and focus only on major spillovers from one jurisdiction to another. Economic development requires freedom for businessmen and for the local authorities that authorize change.

People who value free choice see private vehicles as instruments of choice. Automobiles give people options as to where they live, where they work, and what they do with their free time. Advocates of choice will want to instruct the planners to develop a network of streets and highways.

ACCENTUATE PRESERVATION

If the goal is preservation of the countryside, regional planners will be instructed to focus on control of enterprises (and households) and control of local government agencies that might be too responsive to local initiatives.

Those who want to protect farm and forest land are skeptical of markets. They see them only as institutions that serve self interest. They believe that markets must be controlled.

People who dislike markets also dislike automobiles. They prefer mass transit. Environmentalists want the planners to "tame the automobile," that is, tame the people who drive cars. Travel by auto is to be discouraged and slowed down. Pedestrians and bicycles are to be encouraged. Transportation will be multi-modal. Finally, in order to constrain drivers, shopping centers are to be discouraged, and planners are to design areas of mixed use. Residents must bike or walk to nearby shops rather than drive to a mall.

SITE-SPECIFIC REGIONAL MAPS

Ultimately, land-use planners draw up maps, and their maps do more than identify locations of cities, highways, lakes, and streams. The maps people buy in stores tell them how to get about. The maps they pick up in planning offices tell them where they must locate their activities and structures. They show individuals and firms what they can do in particular locations, but also indicate what they may not do. The map of a planning authority is prescriptive and delineates a set of constraints.

Conflict between those who want choice and growth and those who want to preserve greenspace will lead to different site-specific planning maps. Those who advocate free choice and economic development will want maps of greenbelts and satellite communities or checkerboard maps with public parks scattered out amongst private greenspace. Preservationists will offer maps of compact cities set in a countryside of governmentally-mandated greenspace.

BALANCE AND COMPROMISE

In a mixed economy, the only outcome that seems viable is one that balances diverse interests and concerns. Regional planning in a mixed economy must seek balance between the free choice of households and enterprises and the controls of community. Balance will be hard to achieve. The parties will have to compromise. The culmination of deliberations will be neither as spontaneous as advocates of unfettered enterprise would like to see nor as tidy as the advocates of control would prefer.

On the biggest issues, a Regional Planning Authority not seldom has to give way to locally-elected politicians. The elected politicians deal, and compromise. "We will agree to a destination resort in our area if you will accept a shopping center in yours."

PORTLAND METRO

The best place to look at regional planning in Oregon is in and around its biggest city, Portland. Like the state

Land Conservation and Development Commission, the emphasis of the Portland Metro Council is on preservation. A "livable region," in its view, is one that promotes "a life in nature." To be sure, the Council asserts that Metro values vibrant cities and a healthy diversified economy that provide family wage jobs. The desirability of growth seems to be recognized. But the "adopted growth concept" is "the preservation of natural areas and farm lands." The regional plan is to "actively reinforce the protection of lands currently reserved for farm and forest uses." [1]

What a curious idea, preservation as a source of growth! Economists usually think of growth as something like an increase in gross domestic product per capita. Along this line, Metro might have chosen a growth concept like the best way to use land resources so as to increase the standard of life of people in the Metro area. Little interested in the values created by economic development, however, Metro concerns itself mostly with the *problems* associated with growth.

Metro favors compact development and intends to increase densities within the UGB; development is to occur on infill lots. [2]

To be sure, in accordance with state law, Metro designates "urban reserves" that contain a 30-year supply of buildable land just outside the current Urban Growth Boundary (UGB). Using these reserves, the metropolitan region is to manage its growth. [3]

Outside the UGB, Metro designates "rural reserves" that will help keep communities separate. [4]

Metro designs (maps) the shape of the area under its jurisdiction. It designates centers: Portland as the hub, regional centers (like Gresham and Beaverton), town centers (Cedar Mill, Oak Grove), and neighborhood centers (around light rail stations and other intersections). Transportation corridors of light-rail and highways (on which there will be bus service) are to connect regional centers. Growth, with increased densities, is to take place in centers and along corridors.[5]

Transportation is to be multi-modal (light-rail, buses, autos, bicycles, and pedestrian). The emphasis is to be on mass transit, bicycles, and walking, and the goal is to minimize use of the automobile.[6]

The Metro Council states that "we value the greatest possible individual liberty in politics, economics, lifestyle, belief and conscience . . ." and asserts that "we need to plan for growth in a way that preserves people's ability to choose their own lifestyle."[7] But, if its goal is to create compact cities, and if private open space is not valued, then people will not be free to choose a low-density lifestyle. And, if automobiles are to be discouraged, the choices that are associated with travelers in the private automobile will not be available.

Perhaps most striking in the Metro vision is the Metro Council's failure to recognize the role of private initiative in growth. It seems to believe that the decisions that count are the ones that are made collectively. Growth is to be managed. Yet change, growth, occurs when individuals go off on their own. The static consequences of governmental planning have been demonstrated throughout the world, in the democratic socialisms of Western Europe and by the totalitarian regimes of the defunct Soviet sphere. A government that recognized the ubiquity of scarcity and one concerned with the well-being of its population would recognize the role of private enterprise in the creation of wealth. It would develop a growth concept that is something more than preservation of natural areas and farmlands.

Regional planning as manifested in Portland Metro is planning for containment rather than planning for growth. When critics of the environmental agenda look

at Portland Metro, they are sure to wonder whether regional planning elsewhere in the state will simply respond to the agenda of the preservationists.

CHAPTER 17

THE USES OF NATURE, AND ITS PRESERVATION

Nature, pristine nature, is disappearing. As they drain marshes, clear land, lay out roads, dam rivers, and build cities, human beings change the environment so that less and less remains of undisturbed nature.

The population of the world is growing and spreading out — not only spreading out around the globe, but moving out from cities and expanding into surrounding farm and forest lands. Nature is shrinking.

The little undisturbed nature that remains, minimally changed by human activities, is found both on private and public lands.

PRIVATE PROPERTY IN NATURE

Many environmentalists contend that people cannot own nature. But human beings can and do have private property in nature — a bit of nature in a small backyard near the center of a city, more nature on a large lot in the suburbs, and still more on five acres on the outskirts. Individuals in a capitalist economy do have rights of decision with respect to grass, weeds, shrubs, trees, and the like. They have rights to decide what shall be planted, what harvested, what wildlife to welcome in or to fence out.

One of the rights that makes up the bundle of property rights is the right to enter into contracts. A farmer can sell his piece of nature to an urban householder or developer.

Private ownership of land (that includes pieces of nature), along with the ownership of capital, makes possible private enterprise, the production of goods and services for sale, and the creation of jobs for workers. With private property, land is used and not simply preserved for future use. Wealth is created, and an increasing gross domestic product enables consumers and workers to enjoy the fruits of labor, capital and land.

We have, however, already seen how economic development causes problems in urban and suburban environments: spillovers and congestion. One person's actions cause difficulty for people on adjacent lands. People get in each other's way. Newcomers move into new subdivisions, traffic increases on arterial streets, schools and city parks become crowded.

Then, when suburbanites seek to return to nature, they encounter hordes in the hinterland, at state parks, on lakes and rivers, and at destination resorts.

NATURE ON PUBLIC LANDS

The most dedicated seekers of nature move into remote areas to live, into the rural areas of Idaho, Montana, or Wyoming. If they are really determined to escape from nature despoiled by man, they wander to the ends of the earth or fly into outer space (only perhaps to find trash on Mt. Everest or human debris in space).

Most people cannot go so far in their search for unspoiled nature. With a growing population spreading out over the land, the ordinary citizen finds it more and more difficult to get away from it all. Governments try to provide outdoor experiences on public lands in state and national parks — Oregon Parks and Recreation, the United States Forest Service, the Bureau of Land Management. But public areas for outdoor recreation are overrun by people and threaten to become shabby and bare.

Almost of necessity, the authorities restrict access, especially in parks near cities. "Stay on the trails!" "Camp in Designated Areas!" "Apply for a Permit!" People queue up. Limited slots are rationed. Kayakers may have to wait a year or two for permission to run a river.

One way to reduce the pressure on public lands is to charge fees, prices that reduce the demand for nature. (A community concerned about access for the poor could use a means test and issue "park stamps".)

Still, even with all the rules and limits to access, undisturbed nature becomes hard to find. At the extreme, the community might decide to fence off some land and create really inaccessible nature reserves, to be visited only by a few rangers, scientists, and nature writers. The ordinary person would have to settle for knowing that pure nature exists, out there somewhere, or would have to settle for a vicarious experience of nature in magazine articles or documentary movies.

THE INTERMITTENT ENVIRONMENTALIST

Young and idealistic, living in a modest condominium with a green common area, the ordinary citizen is likely to call himself an environmentalist. He likes clean water and air and neat parks, and worries about the habitat of the spotted owl. Caught in a traffic jam, he is sure that there are too many people in the area and not enough nature.

But when the city dweller accumulates enough money, he forgets his environmental catechism and makes a down payment on a large lot in the suburbs or, if he is really flush, he purchases five acres of land outside the city limits.

In his youth, a farmer supports environmental restrictions that keep subdivisions away from his farm. City kids leave gates open or even vandalize buildings. But when this landowner grows old and is ready to retire, he wants to sell out and move to town. One or both parties to the transfer of land from what was mostly nature to a less natural urban use hire attorneys and land-use consultants to get the approvals to subdivide.

Once established in his suburban retreat, the newcomer to the periphery of the city reverts to his environmental stance. He opposes expansions of the area within the Urban Growth Boundary. He votes against annexations. He is likely to take a stand in opposition to a nearby convenience store, although an environmentally correct position would have him support this mixed land use. He worries about crowded schools and crowded parks, and does what he can to keep people from following him into his haven on the edge of the city.

Rural residents are happy to see forest roads closed if they keep hunters away from their lands—unless, that is, the roads lead to their favorite hunting grounds.

The ordinary voter supports the agenda of the environmentalists. Yet his action in the voting booth does not accord with his actions in the market place. He votes for environmental preservation and then he purchases land in an environmentally-sensitive area.

All this provides a cynical view of mankind. But perhaps we should temper our cynicism. Men and women have dual responsibilities. On the one hand, they are responsible for themselves and their families. On the other hand, as citizens they value a green environment for their communities. People are torn between the market in which they satisfy their individual and family preferences and the community through which they seek to satisfy their collective needs.

We, all of us, face a serious dilemma. With a rising population and a declining quantity of undisturbed land, we recognize the value of what is left of pristine nature. Preserving land in its natural state, however, deprives us of its use in the production of goods and services needed by a growing population. The cost in forgone alternatives of dedicating land to nature increases because we need more and more developed land.

MODERATION, AND RESIGNATION

Clearly, the need is for balance, balance between use and preservation. Use some land to satisfy the wants of present-day residents and their children. Preserve other land for the benefit of future generations. Compensate individuals who are asked to give up development rights on behalf of the community.

And recognize, sadly, that on a planet with an increasing population, undisturbed nature will continue to recede.

END NOTES

CHAPTER 1

1. P. Kropotkin, *Fields, Factories and Workshops* (London: Thomas Nelson and Sons, 1912), pp. vii, 151, 417. Peter Hall, *Cities of Tomorrow* (Oxford: Blackwell, 1989), pp. 3, 5, 144–45.

2. Fishman, R., *Urban Utopias in the Twentieth Century* (New York: Basic Books, 1977), p. 190, quoted in Hall, *ibid.*, pp. 207–09.

CHAPTER 2

1. "The Battle for World Power," *The Economist*, October 7, 1995, p. 23.

2. "Summers on Sustainable Growth," *The Economist*, May 30, 1992, p. 65.

3. G. Cornelis van Kooten, *Land Resource Economics and Sustainable Development: Economic Policies and the Common Good* (Vancouver: UBC Press, 1993), p. 98.

4. Goeller and Weinberg, "The Age of Substitutability," *Science* 191(1976): 683, 685; Joel P. Clark and Frank R. Field III, "How Critical Are Critical Materials?" *Technology Review* 88(1985): 42.

5. Goeller and Weinberg, p. 684.

6. Goeller and Weinberg, p. 689.

7. Chris Maser, *Sustainable Forestry: Philosophy, Science, and Economics* (Delray Beach, FL: St. Lucie Press, 1994), pp. 72–74, 89, 281–284.

8. Michael Pollan, *Second Nature: A Gardener's Education* (New York: Dell Publishing, 1991), pp. 32, 114, 230.

CHAPTER 3

1.   Brent Walth, *Fire at Eden's Gate: Tom McCall and the Oregon Story* (Oregon Historical Society Press, 1994), p. 354.

2.   *Ibid.,* pp. 381, 446–47.

3.   *Ibid.,* p. 246.

4.   *Ibid.,* pp. 355, 382, 396, 458.

5.   *Ibid.,* pp. 379, 400–01.

6.   *Ibid.,* p. 429.

7.   Edward J. Sullivan, "The Legal Evolution of the Oregon Planning System," in Carl Abbott, *et al* (eds), *Planning the Oregon Way: A Twenty-Year Evaluation* (Corvallis, Oregon: Oregon State University Press, 1994), p. 55.

8.   *Ibid.,* p. 26.

9.   *Ibid.,* p. 26, 52.

10.   Copies of the forgoing letters, obtained from landowners, attorneys, and land-use consultants, are in my files.

11.   Mitch Rohse, *Land-Use Planning in Oregon* (Corvallis: Oregon State University Press, 1987), p. 6.

CHAPTER 4

1.   Gregg Easterbrook, "Vanishing Land Reappears," *Atlantic Monthly,* July, 1986, p. 19.

2.   Charles C. Mann, "How Many Is Too Many?" *Atlantic Monthly,* February, 1993, p. 62.

3.   *Ibid.*

4. G. Cornelis van Kooten, *Land Resource Economics and Sustainable Development: Economic Policies and the Common Good* (Vancouver: UBC Press, 1993), pp. 218–219.

5. H. H. Krusekopf quoted in M. Mason Gaffney, "Soil Depletion and Land Rent," *Natural Resources Journal* 4(1965): 544.

6. Robert S. Devine, "The Trouble with Dams," *Atlantic Monthly*, August, 1995, p. 68.

7. "Water: Flowing Uphill," *The Economist*, August 12, 1995, p. 36.

8. Mike Naumes, "The Future of Agriculture in Jackson County," Naumes, Inc., Medford, OR.

9. Dewey Rand Jr., *Capital Press*, May 3, 1996, p. 10.

10. American Farmland Trust, Washington, D.C., 1986.

CHAPTER 5

1. Sherry H. Olson, *The Depletion Myth* (Cambridge: Harvard University Press, 1971), pp. 1–2.

CHAPTER 7

1. Gerrit Knaap and Arthur C. Nelson, *The Regulated Landscape: Lessons on State Land Use Planning from Oregon* (Cambridge, Massachusetts: Lincoln Institute of Land Policy, 1992), pp. 58, 61, 65.

2. Arthur C. Nelson, "Oregon's Urban Growth Boundary Policy as a Landmark Planning Tool," in Carl Abbott, et al (eds), *Planning the Oregon Way: A Twenty-Year Evaluation* (Corvallis, Oregon: Oregon State University Press, 1994), p. 35.

3. "Land Conversion Grows in Oregon," *The Mail Tribune*, May 31, 1995., p. 4A.

4. *Capital Press*, June 14, 96, p. 2.

5. *Capital Press*, September 15, 1995, p. 2.

6. *Capital Press*, May 24, 1996, p. 5.

7. Letter to the Editor, *The Mail Tribune*, January 25, 1996, p. 11A.

8. Knapp and Nelson, *The Regulated Landscape*, pp. 50–52.

9. Medford Planning Department. Board of Commissioners, County of Jackson, Ordinance No. 90-8, 1990, *An Ordinance Adopting a Major Amendment to the City of Medford/Jackson County Urban Growth Boundary.*

10. *Oregon Conifer*, May/June, 1996, p. 12.

11. Mike Burton, "Let's Not Wait for More Growth to Implement 2040 Plan," *The Oregonian*, August 31, 1995, p. E9.

12. *Capital Press*, June 14, 1996, p. 2.

CHAPTER 8

1. Portland Metro, *Metro 2040 Framework Update*, Spring/Summer, 1995, pp. 2–3, 10.

CHAPTER 9

1. Robert E. Dickinson, *City and Region: A Geographical Interpretation* (London: Routledge & Kegan Paul, 1964), p. 497.

2. *Metro Region 2040 Update*, Fall, 1994, p. 6.

CHAPTER 11

1.   Brent Walth, *Fire at Eden's Gate: Tom McCall and the Oregon Story* (Oregon Historical Society Press, 1994), p. 314.

CHAPTER 12

1.   *Mail Tribune,* May 15, 1996, p. 1C.

2.   Dave Mazza, "Congestion Pricing: A New Perspective on Transportation Funding," *Oregon Connifer,* July/August 1992, p. 14.

3.   *Lutraq Update,* Vol. 3, No. 1 (Portland: 1000 Friends of Oregon, June, 1996), p. 1.

4.   "Road Building: From Highway to My Way," *The Economist,* November 18, 1995, p. 29.

CHAPTER 14

1.   Peter Hall, *Cities of Tomorrow: An Intellectual History of Urban Planning and Design in the Twentieth Century* (Oxford: Basil Blackwell, 1988), p. 293.

2.   Joseph A. Schumpeter, *Capitalism, Socialism, and Democracy,* Third ed. (New York: Harper & Brothers, 1950), pp. 73–74.

CHAPTER 16

1.   Portland Metro, *Metro 2040 Framework Update,* Spring/Summer, 1995, pp. 2, 9–10.

2.   *Metro 2040 Framework Update,* Spring/Summer, 1995, p. 3. Portland Metro, *Metro 2040 Framework Update,* Fall 1995/Winter 1996, pp. 2–5.

3. *Metro 2040 Framework Update*, Spring/Summer 1995, p. 6. *Metro* 2040 *Framework Update*, Fall 1995/ Winter 1996, pp. 2, 10.

4. *Portland Metro, Metro Region 2040 Update*, Fall, 1994, p. 6.

5. *Metro 2040 Framework Update*, Spring/Summer, 1995, p. 3.

6. *Ibid.*, pp. 3, 11–12.

7. *Ibid.*, pp. 3, 7.

INDEX

Growth *(continued)* failure to use discount rate for, 62; in cities, 119-20; managed, 118, 159; markets promote, 13, 17-18; not on rural land, 120-21; pressures, 30-32, 74-78, 92, 143; role of private property in, 140; slow, 8, 125, 147; urban, 119-120, 125

Henry George, **133-34**, 136-37

Hickory problem, 58

Highest and best use, 31, 120

Hobby farms. *See* Part-time farmers

Housing, affordable, 69, 94, 100-01, 104, 124; multiple-use, 2

Howard, Ebenezer, 5, 89

Ideology, 129-30

Individualism, 1, 69-70, 96-97, 159, 161, 164

Infill, 79; cost of, 81-82

Infrastructure, cost of, 86

Interest rate. *See* discount rate

Irreversible decisions, 47

Jackson County Citizens League (JCCL), **38**, 143, 149

Jackson County, 38, 93, 149, 153

Kennedy round, 138

Kitzhaber, Governor John, 114

Kropotkin, Prince, 5

Kultur-kamp, 4

Land: buy for protection, 2, 69, 99-100; flat, 32, 94; prices of, 94, 121, 163; public, 85; rent, 133-36; rural uses, 62; trusts, 87-88; urban uses, 62

Landowners, 143, 164

LCDC (Land Conservation and Development Commission), **7**, 71-74, 104-05; and development, 62, 114, 118-21; and preservation, 158; and small-scale agriculture, 53-54, 148; failure to use discount rate, 21, 62-63; official Goals of, 40, 55, 75, 120, 145; history of, 7, 32-33, 141, 144; powers of, 33-39, 103, 155; value judgments of, 145-46

Le Corbusier, 5, 84

Leapfrog development, 93

Liberty, Robert, 78

Livability, 103,144-45, 158

Lloyd George, **134-37**

Local governments: respond to pressures, 75; drag their feet, 32; disabled, 37-39

Low density, 3, 5, 34, 89, **96**, 116

Malls, pedestrian, 2-3, 32, **95-96**, 156

Malthusian, 3, 11, **42-46**, 81

Market failure, 56

Market socialism, 111

Markets, 9, 15, 48; do not take spillovers into account, 31; environmentalists do not consider their roles, 28, 40, 57; for farm land, 41-42; for roads, 109-11; for timber, 57; held Malthusian dragons at bay, 22; preserve rural farmland, 101; satisfy individual preferences, 164

Mass transit, **98**, 111, 156